Meet Jesus

John Twisleton

Text copyright © John Twisleton 2011
The author asserts the moral right
to be identified as the author of this work

Published by
The Bible Reading Fellowship
15 The Chambers, Vineyard
Abingdon OX14 3FE
United Kingdom
Tel: +44 (0)1865 319700
Email: enquiries@brf.org.uk
Website: www.brf.org.uk
BRF is a Registered Charity

ISBN 978 1 84101 895 9

First published 2011
10 9 8 7 6 5 4 3 2 1 0
All rights reserved

Acknowledgments
Unless otherwise stated, scripture quotations are taken from the New Revised Standard
Version of the Bible, Anglicised Edition, copyright © 1989, 1995 by the Division of Christian
Education of the National Council of the Churches of Christ in the United States of America,
and are used by permission. All rights reserved. • Scripture quotations taken from the
Holy Bible, New International Version, copyright © 1973, 1978, 1984 by Biblica. Used by
permission of Hodder & Stoughton Publishers, a member of the Hachette Livre UK Group. All
rights reserved. 'NIV' is a registered trademark of Biblica. UK trademark number 1448790. •
Scripture quotations taken from the Holy Bible, Today's New International Version, copyright
© 2004 by Biblica. Used by permission of Hodder & Stoughton Publishers, a member of
the Hachette Livre UK Group. All rights reserved. 'TNIV' is a registered trademark of Biblica.
• Scripture quotations from THE MESSAGE. Copyright © by Eugene H. Peterson 1993, 1994,
1995. Used by permission of NavPress Publishing Group. • Scriptures taken from the New
Jerusalem Bible, published and copyright © 1985 by Darton, Longman and Todd Ltd and les
Editions du Cerf, and by Doubleday, a division of Bantam Doubleday Dell Publishing Group,
Inc. Used by permission of Darton, Longman and Todd Ltd, and Doubleday, a division of
Random House, Inc.

The Lord's Prayer, The Nicene Creed and The Apostles' Creed as they appear in *Common
Worship: Services and Prayers for the Church of England* (Church House Publishing, 2000) are
copyright © The English Language Liturgical Consultation and are reproduced by permission
of the publisher.

The Commandments as they appear in *Common Worship: Services and Prayers for the Church of
England* (Church House Publishing, 2000) are copyright © Archbishops' Council 2000.

'Open Our Eyes'. Words & Music by Robert Cull. © Copyright Universal Music Publishing
MGB Ltd. All Rights Reserved. International Copyright Secured. Used by permission of Music
Sales Limited.

A catalogue record for this book is available from the British Library

Printed in Singapore by Craft Print International Ltd

Meet Jesus

A CALL TO ADVENTURE

John Twisleton

Acknowledgments

I wish to acknowledge some of those who have helped me meet Jesus and continue in his friendship.

My parents Elsie and Greg and my grandmother Eliza provided the earliest Christian influence. This was supplemented by my housemaster, John Dean, and Giggleswick School chaplain, Philip Curtis, who prepared me for confirmation.

My chemical research supervisor, John White, and St John's College Oxford chaplain Eric Heaton played a formative role in getting me thinking, not least theologically.

Fr John Hooper heard my first sacramental confession and did much in my early years to make Jesus real to me. To him and to the Anglican catholic tradition I owe discovery of the awe and wonder behind the sacraments, the reality of the virgin Mary and the saints, as well as the value of confession and spiritual direction.

Eric Ashby, Graham Leonard, Charles Smith and John Teasdale, several monks of the Community of the Resurrection and Community of the Servants of the Will of God, priest brothers of the Company of Mission Priests and Society of the Holy Cross (SSC) helped me discover the visible church as the fullness of Jesus Christ.

I am grateful to the writers Hans Urs von Balthasar, Teilhard de Chardin, Austin Farrer, Thomas Merton, Henri Nouwen, Michael Ramsey, Saint Thérèse of Lisieux, Colin Urquhart, Robert Warren, David Watson and those of the Orthodox Philokalia for their inspiration, as well as the Cursillo, New Wine and Vassula Ryden's True Life in God networks and my associates at Premier Christian Radio.

I acknowledge the way my wife, Anne, continues to inspire me by her own love for Jesus as together we thank him for his influence upon our sons David, John and James and our evolving family.

Finally I thank the many parishioners, students and colleagues I have served and learned from over the years, and Kevin Bennett, Naomi Starkey, Jan Vernon-Smith and my wife, Anne, for suggesting improvements to the book as it evolved.

❖

Preface

'What do you make of Jesus?' That is a question Jesus himself has provoked from the start. He asked it of others: 'Who do you say I am?' Yet when we read the accounts of his life in the Gospels, we find little self-importance in him.

In picking up this book you are demonstrating a fascination with the paradox that is Jesus. That fascination may come out of a desire to make more of him in your spiritual life or you may want assurance about the historical basis of the founder of Christianity and the claims about him.

Is Jesus God? Or has he been hijacked by the Christian Church? Are the creed, sacraments and commandments of Christianity true to Jesus? What spiritual disciplines help people come close to him? These are questions I face day by day as a parish priest engaging with a post-Christian culture, while being rooted myself in the truth that is in Jesus and the belief that truthfulness cannot be disloyal to him and all he stands for.

This book is written out of a passion for Jesus that recognises him as the ultimate 'Yes, but...' man. To me, Jesus is a provocative reality, always cutting me down to size and expanding my vision of God.

Meet Jesus invites you to open your mind, heart and life to him as much as you dare. It shares wisdom gleaned from the faith of the Church through the ages and insights about the impact of that faith on people today as they continue on their journey of life. The book is structured around seven routes to engagement with Jesus: reason, faith, worship, prayer, fellowship, service and witness.

If meeting Jesus were just a one-way quest, my passion for sharing the truth would be groundless, but I write with the conviction that truth is not just something we seek but also someone who seeks us.

'God is faithful; by him you were called into the fellowship of his Son, Jesus Christ our Lord' (1 Corinthians 1:9)

John Twisleton

Contents

Open our eyes, Lord,
we want to see Jesus,
to reach out and touch him
and say that we love him;
open our ears, Lord,
and help us to listen;
open our eyes, Lord,
we want to see Jesus.

ROBERT CULL (BASED ON JOHN 12:21)

Foreword

In my 20s, having my finished my first degree course at Cambridge, I went out to be what was called 'lektor' in the English/American Literature Department of the 'Free University' of West Berlin. It was June 1953 and, as the plane descended to the city, what you saw below still looked like a moon landscape, with thousands of empty windows and endless mounds of rubble. There I was to find myself overwhelmed at times, in spite of the warm friendship of colleagues, by the suffering, guilt and still, sometimes, the despair of so many shattered people. Yet in the midst of it all, I found, in the local church near where I lodged, a remarkable small group of lay people of all ages, with whom I sometimes studied in my spare time, first contemporary German poetry and then, rather to my surprise, leaping out of the page at us, passages from the Bible.

Through the shared life of these people, there emerged for me, as never in my life before, the figure of a wounded and yet raised-up God in person among us, the living and vital presence of Christ as I had never truly known him before, bringing with him an extraordinary realisation of forgivenness and new life in the Spirit. As we went together to vigorous political meetings about an alternative to what the West or the East had to offer, or to places where we cared for the great throngs of refugees, and also as we gathered together around broken bread and poured-out wine, I encountered in this fresh discovery of Jesus, the Christ, an amazingly alive and quickening force for the healing and renewal of oneself and one's community and for growth into a new, full and everlasting way of being.

Thus I learned for the first time that, in the midst of this world, in a shared human life, in the person of Christ, God can meet with us in the divine Spirit, here embodied, enacted and released, as nowhere else. This is still the encounter with God that we all need to find, and be found by, today. I believe that John Twisleton, in this book, can enable us to discover how God can be found as 'God-with-us and for-us' in the person of Christ, and that is why I would commend the book to potential readers with all my heart and soul!

Simon Barrington-Ward

CHAPTER 1

Open your mind: The place of reason

What are the big and important things in life and how do they connect with each other? The cosmos, the human heart, community, goodness, truth, beauty, courage, self-sacrifice— these could all be listed. With our minds we appreciate such big and important concepts. It is no wonder that we are called *homo sapiens*: literally 'wise man'. To be wise is to see what is important and set one's life in that context.

Meeting Jesus is about seeing the big picture, focusing on the big and important things in life. To engage with Jesus expands the mind and heart. It challenges our view of the way the world is, where it is heading and what difference we could make to it. Jesus is the ultimate connector because he offers hope and healing for our inner life, for community life and for the whole broken world. To his followers he is known as the one who provides remedies for all that pulls life apart. When you have discovered this amazing truth, you may feel sad that so many other people have not done so. The whole 'Jesus' question seems, to them, one of life's cul de sacs, associated with narrow-mindedness at best.

My calling as a priest came at a time when I had just completed a doctorate on the forces between the molecular chains in polythene and Teflon. My scientific career engaged with what connects polymer molecules and gives them their coherence and non-stick properties. Like many scientists, I continue to see the rationality of the material world as evidence for a Creator who planned beforehand the connections I discovered in my research.

As I broke off, day by day, from my chemical studies to serve at a weekday evening Eucharist, I began to see and meet Jesus as one who opened my mind beyond chemistry to his working in the whole of the world. At this sacrament I became, and remain, the student of a far vaster realm, into which material bread and wine and the words of a holy book become entry points.

As a Christian, I still attach great importance to reason. I keep on as a student of Jesus, and it is my experience that he is about truth just as much as chemical research is about truth, and more so. Jesus leads me beyond reason, yes, but never against reason. Through him I capture more and more of the ways in which everything in life truly connects—an idea that is best expressed in the prayer of the priest-scientist Teilhard de Chardin:

You have so filled the universe in every direction, Jesus, that from now on it is blessedly impossible for us to escape you... Neither life, whose progress reinforces the hold you have on me; nor death which throws me into your hands; nor the good or bad spiritual powers which are your living instruments; nor the energies of matter, into which you are plunged... nor the unfathomable abysses of space, which are the measure of your greatness... none of these things will be able to separate me from your substantial love, because they are only the veil, the 'species' under which you hold me so that I can hold you.[1]

Meet Jesus: go out of your mind?

According to my GP, in the medical profession the view is that if you speak to God, you are religious; but if you claim that God speaks to you, then you are mentally unbalanced! Before 21st-century women and men can take Jesus seriously, they need to see evidence that reason is on the side of such an engagement. They need evidence that Jesus brings people to their right mind rather than sending them out of it.

Unfortunately, the sort of religious people who generally get in the news make us question the sanity of those who say they have met God. The 9/11 terrorists are among the most dreadful examples of such a mindset. A few minutes' reflection on the history of Christianity can also bring to mind evidence of inhumanity, such as the Crusades of the Middle Ages. On the other hand, there is also evidence of the way sincere religious believers have revolutionised education, healthcare and the rule of law to everyone's advantage.

Religion is like money, sex or power: it can be used for good or evil. Those who do evil in the name of religion discredit themselves but not necessarily their religion. It may be true that Nazi soldiers carried copies of John's Gospel in their rucksacks, allegedly to promote anti-Semitism, but the same Gospel inspired Father Maximilian Kolbe, who courageously died in place of a married man at the hands of the Nazis in Auschwitz.

So, if we look at the impact of Christianity on people through the ages, we can see both good and ill effects. What few people would dispute, however, is Christianity's claim to have a reasonable historical basis—even if the facts about Jesus are open to debate.

These facts are summarised in the second paragraph of the Apostles' Creed: 'I believe in Jesus Christ, God's only Son, our Lord, who was conceived by the Holy Spirit, born of the Virgin Mary, suffered under Pontius Pilate, was crucified, died, and was buried. He descended to the dead. On the third day he rose again. He ascended into heaven and is seated at the right hand of the Father. He will come to judge the living and the dead.' (See the Appendix for the Creed in full.)

I would like to invite you to open your mind to Jesus. This will not mean losing your reason, although it will mean shelving some doubts, facing some questions and opening yourself to an outcome that may reach beyond your mind into your heart and will. It will, above all, be a chance for you to use your mind to study 'the truth that is in Jesus' (Ephesians 4:21, NIV).

As I said in the preface, this book considers a number of ways in which people engage with Jesus Christ. Some start to know Jesus because they are born into a Christian culture that puts Jesus on the map for them. Others start from an awakening of faith that results from some kind of personal revelation of him. Worship, prayer, Christian fellowship, service and witness are all routes by which we can go deeper with Jesus, but our starting point here is what should be reasonable to an impartial observer.

'In science we have been reading only the notes to a poem; in Christianity we find the poem itself,' wrote C.S. Lewis.[2] Scientific reason is a good starting point for us, even if, in later chapters, we will move beyond reason into considering something of the mystic heights of the Christian revelation.

Meeting Jesus means facing obstacles that may be due to our ignorance, our misunderstanding, or the church's distortion of the facts about him—but we have to face the question, 'Are those obstacles due to the fact that his universal and eternal claims on human beings are actually false?'

To help us understand something of the relationship between reason and faith, we shall look at four very important questions that people have always asked about Christ and are still asking today: Did Jesus exist? Does God exist? Did Jesus rise from the dead? What about other religions?

If Christianity is true, meeting Jesus has two sides to it—his side as well as ours. To reflect this, the various sections of this book end with a meditation upon how Jesus might see the question in hand. While it might seem presumptuous to put words into Jesus' mouth, there is sufficient record of his words in scripture to provide a base for such constructs. You are invited either to use them—looking beyond the words of this book to face its subject—or to skip them and keep up your reading momentum.

Did Jesus exist?

'Isn't Christianity just made up?' people ask. I heard the story of an Italian atheist who took his parish priest to court for teaching the existence of Jesus, and the judge refused to rule! The truth is that we cannot prove 100 per cent that any historical figure existed. Even the 18th-century atheist philosopher Rousseau admitted that it would have been a greater miracle for Jesus to have been invented than for him actually to have existed. Another atheist, author H.G. Wells, insisted that we cannot describe the progress of humanity honestly without giving Jesus first place.

Since Christianity became an established religion, the years in Western societies have been counted from the supposed date of Jesus' birth—a fact that has provoked a counter-reaction in our post-Christian culture, with the forsaking of AD (Anno Domini, 'in the year of our Lord') in favour of CE (Common Era). Some people, discomfited by him and the historic power of the church, have tried to push him out of history altogether. For example, in 1975 historian George Wells published his book, *Did Jesus Really Exist?*,[3] in an attempt to substantiate the earlier claims of atheists such as Bertrand Russell regarding not only Christ's divinity but his very existence. Wells attempted to separate the earliest New Testament writings of St Paul from the later Gospel accounts about Jesus, to claim that they are inconsistent with each other and to suggest some kind of conspiracy.

Even if the historicity and factual basis of the New Testament are accepted, people asking for historical evidence of Jesus usually add the stipulaton '… from outside the Bible'. Although there is such evidence, we should nevertheless consider the hundreds of references to Jesus in the New Testament, which is the key source for his existence. The most radical scholars date the accounts of the life of Jesus that we call the Gospels to no later than AD120. Most accept Mark's Gospel and the common texts shared by Matthew and Luke as being written around AD65, ten years after Paul wrote his earliest letter, 1 Thessalonians. In comparison with other documentation in ancient history, such copious records, written only decades after the alleged death of the person they describe, present very strong proof of that person's existence. Take Alexander the Great as an example: he lived three centuries or so before Jesus, and there is much less historical evidence for his existence that dates from so close to his lifetime.

Of course, the existence of historical figures cannot be demonstrated directly, once all the eyewitnesses have died. Evidence for the existence of both Alexander and Jesus comes from the written record of contemporary witnesses and from second-hand accounts. In the case of Jesus, most of the evidence is second-hand, based on the reports of those who knew him—but why should any information at all have survived about Jesus? Convicted criminals are not usually in the vanguard of history, and, given that he lived in a backwater of the Roman Empire, is it not extraordinary that so much writing about him has survived, whether in secular sources or in the New Testament?

The *Annals of Tacitus*, from the turn of the first century, provide an unfavourable report of 'superstitious Christians' from the hand of one of the ancient world's most famous historians.[4] A little later, another historian, Suetonius, mentions the impact of Christ in Rome, saying that 'since the Jews were making disturbances at the instigation of [the so-called] Chrestus' the emperor expelled them from Rome.[5] The first-century Jewish historian Flavius Josephus also wrote about Jesus, in his book *Antiquities*. Although it is a disputed text, the less disputed version says:

About this time there lived Jesus, a wise man, if indeed one ought to call him a man. His conduct was good and he was known to be virtuous. And many people from among the Jews and the other nations became his disciples. Pilate condemned him to be crucified and to die. But those who became his disciples did not abandon his discipleship. They reported that he had appeared to them three days after his crucifixion, and that he was alive; accordingly he was perhaps the Messiah, concerning whom the prophets have recounted wonders.[6]

Pliny the Younger lived from AD62 to around 115 and chronicled a dramatic period of Roman history, which saw a quick succession of emperors (some of whom were murdered) and the eruption of Vesuvius. He mentions, in passing, the early Christian worship of Jesus, the persecution of believers and their high ethical standards.[7] Second-century writer Lucian of Samosata gives a non-believer's perspective on the new movement of Christianity. He writes, 'The Christians, you know, worship a man to this day, the distinguished personage who introduced their novel rites, and was crucified on that account.'[8]

With such written evidence, the argument that Jesus never existed requires a very selective reading of what was self-evident to the wider ancient world, let alone the writers of the New Testament. The internationally renowned Bible scholar and bishop Tom Wright writes, 'It would be easier, frankly, to believe that Tiberius Caesar, Jesus' contemporary, was a figment of the imagination than to believe that there never was such a person as Jesus.'[9] This can be said despite the fact that we may see Tiberius' face on a coin of the period. We have no similar depiction of Jesus, but, in the normal run of history, a Galilean carpenter would not leave the same sort of mark as the Emperor of Rome.

It is far harder to believe that Jesus did not exist than that he did. The story of Jesus has an extraordinary and consistent force about it that is difficult to consign to mere invention.

Meditation

You question whether I ever existed.
Let me question you!
I came as your God to empty myself for you;
I place by my cross the attempt to erase my profile
from the page of history.
This does not alter this truth: both you and I are in history.
I can see you but you cannot see me.
I can see what is right and what is wrong in you.
Are you fearful about my knowledge of you?
Would you cast me aside when I look upon you with love?
I existed, exist and will exist for your sake, awaiting your love.
I came into human existence to cleanse those who will own me
and fit them to share my divine existence and glory.
I see all and love all—so why do you refuse my love?

(SEE PSALM 139; JOHN 3:16; GALATIANS 2:20)

Does God exist?

When we meet Jesus as a historical figure, we are drawn by his words and deeds to a vision of God. This vision has been expressed by the Church as a trinity, in which Jesus Christ is the second person—the Son of God who took on human nature. With his Father, who made the world, and the Holy Spirit, giver of life, the Son exists as one of three persons in a single God, according to Christian belief.

For many people, a major obstacle to engaging with Jesus today is their disbelief in God. As a result, there is a tendency in Western society to try to sever Jesus from any concept of divinity, so that he is seen as a holy man, an image of unselfishness, the one who served others, and so on, rather than as the Son of God. Meeting Jesus is, however, an invitation to engage with him in both his humanity and his divinity. It is also a challenge to face up to the possibility of God's existence and its implications.

In 2007, I conducted a survey of belief, initially in Sussex, through Chichester Diocese, and then more widely via Premier Christian Radio. From 500 responses, my colleague James Dingemans and I assembled seven arguments for the existence of God:

- First, if everything started with the Big Bang (as most scientists now claim)—and everything evolved from that event—who could have caused this event other than someone outside space, time and matter, who created the space, time and matter, called God?
- Second, the intricacies of the earth, set at just the right distance from the sun to sustain life, and the design of animals and human beings, fit together in a remarkable way. They still fit together notwithstanding all efforts to destroy the fit. All of these signs of order and complexity argue for purpose in the universe.
- Third, if there is no God, what instinct tells us what is right and wrong? Why does humanity revolt against sense-less killing? How are we able to recognise good behaviour by humans, such as help given to the stranger without expectation of reward—or evil and wrong behaviour, such as genocide, the sexual abuse of children or the destruc-

tion of infants? Such instincts are further proof that there is a God and that we have been made in his image.

- Fourth, the recognition of the existence of God is common to almost every human society. From ancient Egypt to today's contemporary society, the overwhelming majority of humans have believed in the existence of a God or gods. There is a consistent historical record of instinctive belief in a being who ranks above the hierarchy of human, animal, vegetable and mineral existence. Are all these peoples and societies, in recognising a power beyond that which is human, wrong? Or is it those who say that there is no God, who lean only on their own understanding, who are misguided?

- Fifth, people who believe in God testify to being changed; having helpful encounters with others at the right times and places in answer to prayer; being healed. This is consistent testimony from different persons in different communities and different countries, over the course of thousands of years. It would be ridiculous to think that all were deceiving themselves or others. If people believe that prayers to God have been answered, is this all just random chance and self-delusion? People and communities who are blessed by such encounters are pointers to the reality of God.

- Sixth, holy people have about them a force from beyond themselves that has the capacity to change other people's lives as they encounter them. This is why Pascal wrote that holiness is the church's greatest influence. Similarly, people who are changed by encounters with the beauty of the natural order, great works of art or music, or by the receiving of unmerited forgiveness, often attribute their transformative experience as evidence for a God at work behind surprises and coincidences.

- Seventh, relationships are among the most important things on earth. They point to belief in a personal God. Belief in God is, conversely, the ultimate statement concerning the dignity and calling of human beings created with a purpose and destiny. Faith in a personal God takes people out of themselves, affirming and empowering them to build better human relationships. When belief in God fails, so can faith in humanity. I recall a man who was ordained with me who had become a believer through interpreting his very strong aversion to racist bullying as an instinct implanted in him, a God-given absolute, relating to human beings as beings made in God's image and worthy of honour, made for fellowship and not enmity.[10]

To repeat: in order to make sense of Jesus, we have to put our minds to the question of God's existence. My belief survey showed a variety of arguments for the existence of God: although all of them can be countered, God, by definition, is not a hypothesis that you can prove or disprove by a knock-down argument. How can we ever prove or disprove a being who is outside the observable? If we could observe God, we would be above his level and he would no longer be God.

As Timothy Keller writes, engaging with the problem of evil as a challenge to God:

If you have a God great and transcendent enough to be mad at because he hasn't stopped evil and suffering in the world… you have… a God great and transcendent enough to have good reasons for allowing it to continue that you can't know… you can't have it both ways.[11]

If God exists, he is beyond us and beyond our thinking. The arguments assembled from my survey simply demonstrate how 500 people defend their belief in the existence of God, and those arguments resonate with others set forth throughout history, not least by people who have come to meet with Jesus as Son of God and Saviour.

Meditation

The fool has said in his heart there is no God.
So says the word of God
and I, Jesus, am that Word.
I came to help you disbelieve in false gods.
I am no moral policeman.
I am no insurance policy.
I am no God on contract,
no God made in your image.
I, Jesus, came upon earth to make God known as he is.
In joyful goodness,
in liberating truth,
in powerful love!
God is Jesus-like and in him
there is no un-Jesus-likeness at all!

(SEE PSALM 14:1; 2 CORINTHIANS 5:19)

Did Jesus rise from the dead?

The teachings of Jesus and their originality astounded those who first heard them, and they still astound people today. He commanded us to love God and to love our neighbours as ourselves, and he blessed the peacemakers, the meek and the lowly. He taught us that, being human, we would fail and would need forgiveness and grace to achieve anything.

His teachings brought him rejection and crucifixion, yet Jesus Christ is the only founder of a world religion who has no grave. His resurrection is as well attested as any event in history; the enigmatic tone of the accounts of Easter in the four Gospels would be absent in any made-up tale. The place of women as witnesses to the resurrection—remarkable and controversial at the time—would not have been included in any fabricated story. The new confidence seen among the previously frightened disciples is fully evident after the descent of the Holy Spirit, an event inseparable from the historical event of the resurrection (John 20:19–23; Acts 2:1–36). The transformation of a dejected, defeated group into a band of powerful witnesses to the resurrection would be inexplicable in human terms unless the event they proclaimed (namely that Jesus had risen from the dead) were true.

'This Jesus God raised up,' Peter says in Acts 2:32, and continues, 'God has made him both Lord and Messiah, this Jesus whom you crucified' (v. 36).

The experience of meeting with Jesus is at the heart of Christianity's survival over the last 2000 years. The risen Christ appears like a rainbow in the midst of the storms of life, in the very midst of history, to open up for us the beauty and glory that lie ahead for believers.

Modern mathematics has shown, through so-called chaos theory, that complicated systems such as the weather are chaotic in nature, the result of random events occurring in an infinity of places. Yet, from this chaos can and do emerge very beautiful manifestations of order and pattern, such as rainbows or colourful sunsets. So, argues the Christian mathematician, although the tendency of living forms is towards the greater chaos of death and dissolution, the emergence at one point in time and space of the risen Christ is in harmony with our understanding of the theory of chaos and human existence. The emergence at one point of a man brought back from the dead is in harmony with scientific truth, as much as is the emergence of a beautiful rainbow on a stormy day.

The theologian Karl Rahner spoke of the revolutionary implications of Jesus' resurrection, using the image of a volcano:

What we call Jesus' resurrection—and unthinkingly take to be his own private destiny—is only the first surface indication that all reality, behind what we usually call experience, has already changed in the really decisive depth of things. Jesus' resurrection is like the first eruption of a volcano which shows that God's fire already burns in the innermost depths of the earth, and that everything shall be brought to a holy glow in his light. He rose to show that this has already begun. The new creation had already started.[12]

Harvard law professor Simon Greenleaf had this to say about the varying testimonies to the resurrection of Jesus: 'There is enough of a discrepancy to show that there could have been no previous concert among them; and at the same time such substantial agreement as to show that they all were independent narrators of the same great transaction.'[13] This transaction, as he calls it, is further evidenced in history by the fact that the newly formed Christian Church changed its weekly holy day from the Jewish Sabbath to Sunday, the day of Christ's rising. What a change that would have been for devout Jewish believers!

How could such a frightened bunch of men and women have ended up confronting the authorities so confidently with the news that Jesus was and is alive? Some of them became martyrs, willing to die for their belief that Jesus is Lord. Could you imagine dying for a claim that you know to be false?

Many thousands have read former atheist Lee Strobel's book *The Case for Christ*. Strobel, a journalist and law student, attempted a rigorous investigation of the evidence for Jesus and, as a result, came to faith himself. After studying the accounts of the resurrection appearances of Jesus, Strobel concluded that they were as well authenticated as any event in history. The discrepancies between these accounts—the number and placing of angels, which of the disciples was first at the scene, exactly where Christ appeared and so on— actually provide a ring of truth. These variations are consistent with the recording of a stupendous event. Anyone seriously attempting to make up the resurrection stories would have done a better job of it!

Meditation

*Since I brought all that is out of nothing
and entered the world through a virgin womb,
does it surprise you that I came out of the grave?
I, Jesus, commend to you a God who is no 'genie in a lamp'
but Lord God of power and might.
To meet me is to come into a never-ending friendship.
Nothing can overcome the love of God—not even death!
I died and rose and come to judge;
your spiritual dying and rising prepares you for that judgment.
As I rose, all men and women must rise,
willing or unwilling, to salvation or condemnation.
Resurrection is your lot as it is mine—
but there is no condemnation
for those who die to self and rise in the Spirit
to eternal life in Christ Jesus.*

(SEE ROMANS 8; HEBREWS 1:1–4)

What about other faiths?

If there is an invitation to meet Jesus, how does it stand in relation to the invitations within our global village from non-Christian faiths?

If one faith claims to be universally true, it seems inevitable that it will be at the expense of all the others. Is it a totally black-and-white matter, though? Can we claim that

Christianity is 'right' and every other faith 'wrong'? Holding together the certain claim of Christ with a respect for that which is good and noble and true in other creeds is the challenge of our age, as it was, indeed, for the first age of the Church.

The apostles who preached the risen Christ as unique Son of God and Saviour were also able to bring out a witness to him from the poetry of Greece (Acts 17:22–28). St John was ready to describe Jesus as the one who 'enlightens everyone' (John 1:9). Right from the beginning, holding loyalty to Jesus as the truth has not prevented Christians from recognising what is true in other creeds as being also of him, since all truth ultimately comes from the same divine source.

The Anglican bishops who assembled for the 1988 Lambeth Conference affirmed, 'Anything that is "exclusively" true of the incarnate Lord is true of one who is precisely the most "inclusive" reality, the divine life rejoicing in itself and seeking to share itself.'[14] In other words, the safeguarding of Jesus' uniqueness as the way to God defends the vision of a God who is present both over all and personally to all, a vision that is ultimately inclusive and not exclusive.

There is something about Jesus that transcends Christianity as a religion. This was also acknowledged by Roman Catholic bishops at the Second Vatican Council (1962–65) in their declaration on other faiths:

The Catholic Church rejects nothing which is true and holy in these religions. She looks with sincere respect upon those ways of conduct and of life, those rules and teachings which, though differing in many particulars from what she holds and sets forth, nevertheless often reflect a ray of that truth which enlightens all men [sic]. Indeed she proclaims and must ever proclaim Christ 'the way, the truth, and the life' (John 14:6), in whom men [sic] find the fullness of religious life, and in whom God has reconciled all things to Himself (cf. 2 Corinthians 5:18–19).[15]

Saying 'yes' to Jesus does not mean saying 'no' to everything about other faiths. It can mean saying 'yes, but…' to other faiths, which is a far more engaging and reasonable attitude. I say 'yes' to what Buddhists teach about detachment, because Jesus teaches it and Christians often forget it. At the same time, I must respectfully question Buddhists about their lack of a personal vision of God, since I believe that Jesus is God's Son. I say 'yes' to what Muslims teach about God's majesty, because sometimes Christians seem to domesticate God and forget his awesome nature. At the same time, I differ with Muslims about how we gain salvation, because I believe that Jesus is God's salvation gift and more than just a prophet.

Other faiths can wake us up to aspects of Christian truth that might otherwise get forgotten. What might happen if Christians were as serious in their spiritual discipline as many Buddhists are? What might happen if Christians knew their Bible as well as many Muslims know the Koran, and were as committed to seeing the values of their faith respected in wider society?

Thank God, the Christian faith points not to its own truth so much as to Jesus—whose truth is bigger than any religion. Ultimately, being a Christian is about a relationship, not adherence to a set of beliefs. This is what Jesus means when he says, 'No one comes to the Father except through me' (John 14:6b) or what Paul means when he writes that Jesus has 'the name that is above every name' and that 'every tongue should confess that Jesus Christ is Lord' (Philippians 2:9, 11).

It is arguable that the existence of other faiths is proof of the failure of Christians to meet with Jesus at a deep level and so to become, through his magnetic love, the means of drawing others to the heart of God.

Meditation

He who is not against me is for me.
If you meet with me,
you will be joining an extraordinary company.
My friends are inside and outside my Church.
I am the light that lightens everyone who comes into the world,
and something of my light can be found in many world faiths.
I am the way, the truth and the life;
no one comes to God except through his Son, Jesus Christ.
This is beyond human reason—
my thoughts are higher than that.
I, Jesus, call people to turn to me and be saved!

(SEE ISAIAH 45:22–25; 55:6–9; JOHN 1:9; 14:6)

In summary

Meeting Jesus is a mind-expanding business. Although he takes us beyond reason, Jesus tells us that he is about truth, which should not contradict reason. Nevertheless, many people suspect that getting involved with Jesus, or any sort of faith, is to get mixed up with irrationality and narrow-mindedness. For them, it is unclear whether following Jesus leads to being right-minded or simply narrow-minded.

There is a reasonable consensus that Jesus existed, drawn from both non-Christian and Christian documentation. That Jesus rose from the dead is a reasonable belief, given the historical evidence. Jesus points us to God, whose existence can be argued to be reasonable, even if meeting Jesus as God's Son requires faith alongside reason.

Saying 'yes' to Jesus does not mean saying 'no' to everything about other faiths. The Christian attitude to other faiths can be 'yes, but...', which itself is a reasonable attitude.

Thinking through the facts about Jesus that people dispute today is a fruitful exercise. Opening our minds to what Jesus could represent helps to clear the ground for engaging with him at other levels—if that is what we want to do.

For action
- Identify whatever it is that you find confusing about Jesus, and attempt to clarify the issues.
- Reflect upon the order and beauty of creation and its significance.
- Try to evaluate for yourself whether Jesus rose from the dead or not, by reading the endings of the four Gospels. (See also N.T. Wright, *Jesus and the Victory of God*.)
- Find out more about other faiths, and research what books and the internet have to say about Christianity. (See *The World's Religions*, edited by Christopher Partridge, for a good starting point.)[16]

CHAPTER 2

Open your ears: The place of faith

One of the ways our minds get fed is through our ears: we could describe the way to our heart as via the 'inner ear' that we call faith. Taking on all that Jesus has for us requires a capacity that goes beyond reason. When we look at the historical facts about Jesus, they are reasonable up to a point, but making sense of his teaching is another matter. What sense can there be, for example, in his promise that 'those who find their life will lose it, and those who lose their life for my sake will find it' (Matthew 10:39)?

Meeting Jesus is an uncomfortable challenge to self-interest. There is something far- and deep-reaching about him. He reaches out through the centuries and across the globe, touching the hearts of people of every race and nation. He calls us to a self-surrender that goes beyond and arguably against reason.

Saint Francis of Assisi found his values turned upside down by the scriptural invitation to 'lose his life', which he took as advice for his life there and then. As a result, he surrendered his inheritance, even exchanging his clothes for sackcloth, to live with Jesus in holy poverty, and he started a movement for simplicity that had a great impact on his own age and on later centuries. When people recognise God's word in Jesus, they find that the one who originally gave them life reaches down to plant his resurrection life in their open hearts and bring them a new start.

As the Nicene Creed tells us: 'For us and for our salvation he came down from heaven, was incarnate from the Holy Spirit and the Virgin Mary and was made man' (see Appendix). Christian faith sees the historical Jesus in the wider context of God's self-revelation, once and for all, reaching out through the ages to commune with those whom the Spirit has gifted with faith in him.

There can be few people who have not heard of Jesus at all—at least as the founder figure of one of the world's largest religions. What they do with this knowledge will be determined by their attitude to faith in general and Christianity in particular, and any encounters they have with those who claim to have met Jesus at a deeper level will colour that attitude further.

When I was a child, my picture of Jesus was shaped by my parents and those who taught me at Sunday school. It was coloured by kind, unselfish people I met, who cherished Christ. There came a day, though, when I realised that although I had been baptised as a child, I needed to choose to profess faith in Christ myself. I decided to get confirmed and personally own the faith of the Christian church to which my parents had committed me at my birth. Through my confirmation classes, I heard with my reason, my 'outer ear', about the creed, sacraments, commandments and spiritual disciplines of Christianity. I also sensed a little unblocking of my 'inner ear' of faith as Jesus began to reveal himself more fully to me, especially in the sacrament of his body and blood.

The rational mind can take us to Jesus, like the proverbial horse to water, but it cannot make us drink of him. For that, we need faith. As Pope John Paul II wrote, 'Faith and reason are like two wings on which the human spirit rises to the contemplation of truth.'[17] Without the gift of faith, we reason Jesus down to a level we can tolerate. We conform him to ourselves—but the real business should be to conform ourselves to him.

Meeting Jesus is about meeting and befriending God, and that can never be on our terms alone. God gives us, in Jesus, a capacity to be one with him, which not only challenges but can actually uproot self-centredness. This can look and feel pretty 'unreasonable'! Nevertheless, the faith to which Jesus calls us complements our rational understanding, so that we can live our lives open to the possibilities of God that pass human imagining.

What is faith?

A story is told of an acrobat who pushed his son in a wheelbarrow as part of his high-wire act. When spectators asked his son how he felt about the exercise, his only comment was, 'I trust my dad.' Here is faith defined almost as a 'sixth sense', quite beyond the natural senses but, nevertheless, based on experience. The boy needed no explanation for the faith he had in his father, although few others would rise to it. 'To one who has faith, no explanation is necessary. To one without faith, no explanation is possible,' wrote Thomas Aquinas, the 13th-century philosopher-priest.

Holding a faith in Jesus means holding the certain conviction that you will be carried forward, through all the perils of life, by one who loves you beyond reason, who died for you. In the words of St Paul, 'I live by faith in the Son of God, who loved me and gave himself for me' (Galatians 2:20b).

To hear God's voice in the voice of Jesus requires an unblocking of the 'inner ear' of faith, and this can happen suddenly or bit by bit. Paul's faith in Christ came in a blinding flash when he met Jesus on the road to Damascus (Acts 9:3–9). For others, meeting Jesus is a slow journey in which reason, faith, worship, prayer, fellowship, service and witness play their part in building the friendship.

The first person to profess faith in Christ was Simon Peter. We read this telling account in the middle of Matthew's Gospel:

Now when Jesus came into the district of Caesarea Philippi, he asked his disciples, 'Who do people say that the Son of Man is?' And they said, 'Some say John the Baptist, but others Elijah, and still others Jeremiah or one of the prophets.' He said to them, 'But who do you say that I am?' Simon Peter answered, 'You are the Messiah, the Son of the living God.' And Jesus answered him, 'Blessed are you, Simon son of Jonah! For flesh and blood has not revealed this to you, but my Father in heaven.' (Matthew 16:13–17)

Jesus is clear that seeing him as he really is requires a personal revelation from God. When Nicodemus praised Jesus for his miraculous signs, Jesus made the same point, replying, 'Very truly, I tell you, no one can enter the kingdom of God without being born of water and Spirit' (John 3:5). As Charles Wesley's Christmas carol puts it, Jesus was 'born to raise the sons of earth, born to give them second birth'. The 'inner ear' that is faith comes as a gift of the Spirit, who is inseparable from Jesus and his Father. Meeting with Jesus accomplishes the heavenly second birth into the realm of the Holy Spirit.

Augustine of Hippo is one of the most famous Christian

writers. He lived in the fourth century and experienced a dramatic opening of the heart to Jesus. He had come under the influence of the saintly bishop Ambrose of Milan and was taking time out from his work to reflect upon his life. Sitting in the garden, he heard children playing next door, singing the repeated chorus '*Tolle et lege*', the Latin for 'Take up and read'. Augustine took this as a direct word from God, picked up his New Testament and read immediately the invitation to 'put on the Lord Jesus Christ' (Romans 13:14). He did so, quitting his teaching position in Milan and throwing himself entirely into the service of God. The rest of his life was spent in interpreting scripture as a preacher and writer.[18]

'Faith comes from what is heard' (Romans 10:17). Meeting Jesus involves opening our ears to hear who he is, what he has said and what he has done for us, especially as recorded in scripture. Our faith grows as we seek him not only with our intellect but in a stage-by-stage surrender of the will to him, so that his life takes deeper and deeper root in ours. This vital act of surrender is captured in Thomas Aquinas' famous definition of faith: 'Believing is an act of the intellect assenting to the divine truth by command of the will moved by God through grace.'[19]

Meditation

I yearn for you to know me
and love me as I love you.
Though I, as God, am different from you,
I am also the same—

I know your human condition through and through,
having created it,
and being Jesus, 'a man of sorrows, acquainted with grief'.
I pray for you the gift of faith so we can speak one to one,
the assurance of things hoped for, the conviction of things unseen.
By faith, I who am invisible can be reached
and touched by longing love.
The magnetic force of my love is set to draw all with faith
to my delights.
I, Jesus, am God made visible, inviting mortals to faith,
by which alone they can please me
and be caught up into love of the God they cannot see.

(SEE ISAIAH 53:3; JOHN 12:32; 1 JOHN 4:19)

What Jesus did

God came to earth in Jesus, who took human form through the virgin Mary, to die and then be raised, lifting believers to glory. This is what Christians believe: God is 'downwardly mobile' because he loves us!

Thomas Merton compared this coming of God to the sun shining through a magnifying glass. Just as a magnifying glass concentrates the rays of the sun into a little burning knot of heat that can set objects on fire, so the coming of Christ concentrates the ray of God's light and fire to such a point that it sets fire to the human spirit.[20]

When we approach Jesus with faith in his divinity, we recognise that his crucifixion stands at the climax of human history. It is seen as a great act of substitution in which Jesus died in our place so that he can live in our place. The holiness of God, affronted by sin, demands a penalty, which he himself provides. The shedding of the blood of God's Son, Jesus Christ, fulfils ancient sacrificial rites by providing a sinless offering who alone can expiate sin. As we read in Ephesians 5:2, Christ loved us, 'giving himself up for us as an offering and a sweet-smelling sacrifice to God' (NJB).

To believe in the crucifixion of Jesus is to commit to a God who loves us and is holy, who reaches out to us in love even though we are sinners. In his holiness he cannot be reconciled to sin (Habakkuk 1:13a), but, through the sacrifice of Jesus upon the cross, the horror of sin is overcome and we are credited with God's own love and holiness. The power of evil over humankind is overcome by the cross, such that Christ has been likened to a triumphant general who leads believers in his victory procession (2 Corinthians 2:14).

As we have seen, it is impossible to weigh up rationally the historical figure of Jesus without evaluating the claim that he rose from the dead, which takes centre place in the Christian creed: 'On the third day he rose again according to the scriptures' (see Appendix). The experience of the living Christ and the benefits he brings to us by his death is at the heart of the survival and spread of Christianity over the past 2000 years.

To the eye of faith, it is the resurrection that demonstrates Jesus' uniqueness. A former Lord Chief Justice, Lord Darling, wrote, 'In its favour there exists such overwhelming evidence, positive and negative, factual and circumstantial, that no intelligent jury in the world could fail to bring in a verdict that the Resurrection story is true.'[21] This is a legal response to the idea of the resurrection, but there are also positive responses from science to this great exception to the laws of nature. Priest and scientist John Polkinghorne has studied the parallels between physics and theology, insisting that both realms have surprises—exceptions that prove the rules. He points out that Ohm's Law, which predicts the resistance of metals to electric current, breaks down at very low temperatures, when metals become superconductors. In the same way, when a man is dead and buried, but is also God's Son, there is an exception to the laws of nature.[22] This exception we call the resurrection, which is God's signature on all that Jesus lived and died for.

To argue that dead people do not rise again, and so Jesus could not have risen, is to reject any possibilities beyond this world. To accept that Jesus both died and rose is to accept such possibilities for him, for ourselves and for all who seek the truth about Jesus.

What happened to the historical figure of Jesus during the 33 years of his earthly life speaks, to the ear of faith, a word from God the Creator. 'The Word became flesh and lived among us, and we have seen his glory, the glory as of a father's only son, full of grace and truth... No one has ever seen God. It is God the only Son, who is close to the Father's heart, who has made him known' (John 1:14, 18). The earthly life of Jesus is a call to faith in the invisible God, made known in acts of forgiveness, healing and compassion. There is an integrity about Jesus, a unique matching of words and deeds, that points beyond himself and invites us to put faith in his heavenly Father. That integrity was fully demonstrated by his readiness to lay his life on the line, dying and rising so that, in meeting him, we can die to sin and rise to new life. To believe as a Christian is to accept what God has done through Jesus—a work of God unique in the history of the universe—and to be humbled by it.

Even the most sceptical atheist will not deny Jesus Christ a place in history, but for believers he is more than an historical figure. History is *his* story!

Meditation

It is called the scandal of the particular.
Why should a particular life lived in a particular age
be set apart for universal significance?
I, Jesus, am the same yesterday, today and always,
living in the power of an indestructible life
to bring God to human beings and human beings to God.
The scandal—or stumbling block—is this:
though death is universal, my Love is also universal
and beyond both life and death.
To gain the world's attention to my coming in flesh,
that flesh was glorified once it lay in death.
What usually happens usually happens—but not always.
My possibilities exceed human imagining
as surely as my life is beyond that of mortals.

(SEE 1 CORINTHIANS 15:52; EPHESIANS 3:20; HEBREWS 7:15–17)

Baptism in the Spirit

What Jesus did long ago is made relevant today by the Holy Spirit. John the Baptist said, 'I have baptised you with water; but [Jesus] will baptise you with the Holy Spirit' (Mark 1:8). We cannot meet Jesus and take on his demands—to pray, to love, to serve, to evangelise, to be obedient, to forgive, to heal—without the help of his Spirit.

The invitation to self-sacrifice in the message of Jesus is

clear: 'Those who find their life will lose it, and those who lose their life for my sake will find it' (Matthew 10:39). This invitation is mercifully accompanied by promises like these: '"Whoever believes in me, as Scripture has said, rivers of living water will flow from within them." By this he meant the Spirit, whom those who believed in him were later to receive' (John 7:38–39, TNIV) and 'You will receive power when the Holy Spirit has come upon you; and you will be my witnesses' (Acts 1:8). In the days of his earthly life, and since then, Jesus has met with people who have shrunk from the cost of following him. Where people face the cost, however, they discover that Jesus is always ready to empower them by releasing the flow of his Spirit into their lives.

It is clear from scripture that baptised Christians possess the Holy Spirit. We possess the Spirit—but do we truly allow him to possess us? That is the key to spiritual vitality. Note that, in scripture, this never means possession in the literal sense; rather, the sense is of cooperation. When the Holy Spirit came upon the virgin Mary, the gift was associated with her promised cooperation (Luke 1:38). Our renewal in the Holy Spirit, like her anointing, is about the releasing of the Spirit within us.

Over my years as a priest, I have regularly visited Lourdes. It is a wonderful place of healing, set in magnificent scenery on the lower slopes of the Pyrenees in France. In the story of Lourdes the key figure is a peasant girl, Bernadette, a shepherdess who in 1858 received a number of visions, allegedly of the virgin Mary. In one of these visions, she was asked to dig down and lift some earth, uncovering a spring that flows to this day, a healing stream visited by millions every year.

How important discernment is! What healing streams can

flow from one little insight! Sometimes we who have met with Jesus in word and sacrament over many years need to be shown blockages that need lifting, so that our spiritual life can be invigorated and a fresh vision of Jesus opened up.

The late Dom Ian Petit of Ampleforth Abbey wrote:

Baptism and Confirmation confer a supernatural gift, but ignorance or lack of understanding of the gift can block its full effect. In other words, while the sacrament is valid and has been given, the effect has been blocked. When the block is removed then the full effect floods in… a baptism in the Holy Spirit… an opportunity for awakening in people their sacraments of initiation.[23]

My own sense of empowerment in the Spirit relates to the lifting of the stone of unbelief. By that stage in my life, I was definitely committed to Jesus. I had received baptism, confirmation and ordination. I regularly welcomed Jesus in the sacraments of confession and communion. Shortly after I was ordained priest, however, I had a real crisis of faith. I went back on a sort of retreat to the Community of the Resurrection at Mirfield, where I had trained. It was a chance to work out what should happen next, since I hardly believed in the reality of God any more. While there, I was taken under the wing of Father Daniel, one of the monks of the Community. He gave me this advice: 'Maybe, John, it is not Jesus who's gone but your vision of him. Why not pray an honest prayer, like, "Lord, if you're there, show yourself. Give me a vision of yourself that's to your dimensions and not mine."' With nothing to lose, I prayed Fr Daniel's prayer and waited, for probably the most difficult and cliff-hanging two days of my life.

Then Jesus answered. He chose a leaf on a tree in the

monastery garden. I was walking along with no particular thought in my head when my eyes fell on the leaf—and it was as if it spoke to me. 'He made you,' the leaf seemed to say.

I was bowled over. As I moved forward, I saw the great crucifix that stands in the rockery. 'I made you. I love you,' the figure of Jesus seemed to say.

'Father, Son... what about the Holy Spirit?' My mind was spinning. The Father was saying, 'I made you', the Son, 'I love you.' Could it be that the Spirit was saying, 'I want to fill you'? A group of Mirfield Fathers prayed for me to be filled afresh with the Holy Spirit—and from that day forward, Jesus has seemed much closer to me, in his word as well as sacrament, in people and nature as well as in church.

Since that deepening experience in the Holy Spirit, I have felt a greater wholeness or integration between what I believe, say, pray and do—how I live my life. Before, what I believed and the way I lived my life seemed less integrated. Thirty years later, I am still, of course, seeing my beliefs and my life continue to draw closer together. Looking back, I can recognise that my meeting with Jesus has been transformative. He lifted a stone of unbelief that was blocking the release of his Spirit. He opened my life and my ministry to a new movement forward, which included mission work overseas in Guyana.

I have come to recognise the vital role of expectant faith, without which people miss out on the empowerment of the Holy Spirit—one of the greatest gifts of Jesus to both individuals and communities. Looking at the life of Jesus, we see that he himself, although conceived by the Holy Spirit, waited 30 years for his baptism in the Holy Spirit in the River Jordan. So it can be, as it was for me, that although we receive the Spirit through infant baptism, confirmation and (for some of us) ordination, the first deeply personal experience comes many years later—through, of all things, a crisis of faith and a recommitment.

Another way to look at it is this: if the Christian life is like a rose bush, there are great spurts of growth from time to time that push out new branches with new flowers. One such branch (and it is quite some branch in its fruitfulness) is, if you like, a new opening up to the Spirit. Yet the life of the rose bush before and after such a new spurt of growth is the same life.

You may possess the Spirit—but does he possess you? That is the question Jesus would ask of many in his Church today. For any who are heavily burdened in some way, Jesus invites us to take courage, to lift the stones of unbelief or unforgiveness or stubbornness and open ourselves up to the wellsprings of the Spirit that he has promised us.

Meditation

Without the Holy Spirit, God is far away,
Christ stays in the past,
the Gospel is a dead letter,
the Church is simply an organisation,
authority a matter of dominion,
mission a matter of propaganda,
the liturgy no more than an evocation,
and Christian living a slave mentality.

But in the Holy Spirit:
the cosmos is resurrected
and groans with birthpangs of the kingdom,
the risen Christ is there,
the Gospel is the power of life,
the Church shows forth the life of the Trinity,
authority is a liberating service,
mission is a Pentecost,
the liturgy is both memorial and anticipation,
and human action is deified.[24]

The Trinity

Meeting Jesus is a two-way process in which faith reaches to God in eager longing and God's Spirit anoints the seeker. As in any friendship, there is a gradual revelation of one self to another. In the case of Jesus, we are talking about an invisible figure whose capacity to reach down to us through history derives from the resurrection. As he reveals himself, furthermore, we are caught up into relationship with God—Father, Son and Holy Spirit.

Although we know that Jesus was born in Bethlehem, his early years are not well documented at all. The account of his adult life in the four Gospels starts with his baptism, as in St Luke's account:

Now when all the people were baptised, and when Jesus also had been baptised and was praying, the heaven was opened, and the Holy Spirit descended upon him in bodily form like a dove. And a voice came from heaven, 'You are my Son, the Beloved; with you I am well pleased.' Jesus was about thirty years old when he began his work. He was the son (as was thought) of Joseph son of Heli… son of Adam, son of God. (Luke 3:21–23, 38)

In this account of the start of Jesus' ministry when he was aged around 30, we read of two signs that point to his origin and destination in God, the Holy Trinity. There is a voice, presumed to be that of God the Father, affirming his divine Sonship. There is also a descent of the Holy Spirit, seen as a dove. We could say that from then on, Jesus becomes Jesus Christ, which means literally Jesus the 'anointed one'. This early incident is the first revelation of the Trinity.

As Jesus is anointed Christ at his own baptism, he receives the Spirit, with the intent of bestowing it on all baptised Christians, as John the Baptist states: 'He on whom you see the Spirit descend and remain is the one who baptises with the Holy Spirit. And I myself have seen and have testified that this is the Son of God' (John 1:33–34). To meet Jesus as a Christian is to share the anointing he has as the Christ, or 'Spirit-anointed one'. It is to be drawn into the love he has for God his Father in the unity of the Holy Spirit, demonstrated by his death and rising again. This is why Christian baptism is 'in the name of the Father and of the Son and of the Holy Spirit'.

Belief in the Trinity is the logical outcome of the revelation of God that Christians have recognised. We believe that God is one in himself but we have to reckon with Jesus and the Spirit because we have seen them at work. If God had never come to earth in Jesus, for example, there would be no talk of God as three in one. We believe that God acts in three persons but we cannot believe that God is disunited. That is why we say that God is not one God or three Gods but three persons in one God.

Only when we talk of love does the mystery of the Trinity make sense. God is love in himself, the love of Father and Son in the Holy Spirit who is their go-between. This explains how love can exist without anything to love, how it can have existed before the creation of the world. What trinitarian doctrine is out to defend is the revelation of God as personal relationship. If Christianity is true, ultimate reality has got a heart. As Christians see it, those who deny the Trinity, such as Unitarians, actually depersonalise God, making him more remote and irrelevant.

Many people have wondered why there is no mention of the Trinity in the Bible. In fact, although we do not find the word in scripture, we do see the reality. Believers talk of themselves as being like Jesus, as being children of God the Father and as sharing his anointing in the Holy Spirit. It is by the Spirit, scripture teaches, that we call God our Father and Jesus our Lord (Romans 8:15b; 1 Corinthians 12:3b). By faith we meet Jesus, seeking 'the grace of the Lord Jesus Christ, the love of God and the communion of the Holy Spirit' (2 Corinthians 13:13). The biblical teaching is that we cannot meet Jesus, apart from engaging with the whole of God.

Meditation

No one fully comprehends what is truly mine except my Spirit.
As you meet me in Jesus, you partake of the Spirit.
I can say of you, as I have said of Jesus:
You are my beloved child.
I am well pleased with all who have faith.
You are destined to share my life,
that of Father, Son and Holy Spirit.
May you have power to comprehend,
with all the saints,
what is the breadth and length
and height and depth,
and to know the love of Christ
that surpasses knowledge,
so that you may be filled with all my fullness.

(SEE 1 CORINTHIANS 2:11; EPHESIANS 3:18–19; HEBREWS 11:6)

Holy Scripture

'Jesus loves me, this I know, for the Bible tells me so' runs the old chorus. If we want to build friendship with Jesus, getting to know holy scripture is essential. 'Let the word of Christ dwell in you richly,' Paul wrote to early Christian believers; 'teach and admonish one another in all wisdom' (Colossians 3:16).

To many people, meeting Jesus sounds more engaging and

personal than reading the sizable library of books assembled in scripture that we call the Bible (from the Greek *biblia*, which means 'library'). We need a guide, and that guide is actually provided by Jesus, through his Holy Spirit and also his Church.

Jesus is the definitive Word of God (John 1:1) who opens our ears to hear the promise of salvation recorded in the Bible. People fail to understand the relevance of holy scripture until their ears are opened by repentance and they turn their attention away from the many things that drive them in life, choosing instead to make Jesus their key inspiration. Building a deep relationship with the Lord is impossible without day-by-day repentance from selfish pursuits, which also opens our 'inner ears' to understand that 'all scripture is inspired by God and is useful for teaching, for reproof, for correction, and for training in righteousness' (2 Timothy 3:16). As people repent, they receive scripture's great connector to human life—the Holy Spirit, who gives life to the Christian Church. He is the one who helps people open up to the Bible as the life-changing book it is.

God has revealed himself in Jesus—this is the heart of Christianity—and holy scripture holds before us both the record and the ongoing impact of that revelation. The Bible points us to what Jesus has done for us by his death and resurrection and holds us to him. When we meet Jesus and put faith in him, we begin to see our life as part of the Bible story. We find purpose and belonging in this world and hope for the world to come.

Approached with an open heart, scripture brings hope and encouragement. Approached with argumentative pride, it presents a different picture. Let me repeat: the Bible's relevance dawns when the Holy Spirit opens humble seekers to its divine wisdom, hidden in human words. People who take God at his word in the promises of scripture see Jesus changing their life by that same Spirit.

On 24 May 1738, Methodist pioneer John Wesley opened his Bible at 2 Peter 1:4 and read of God's 'precious and very great promises' through which we 'may become participants in the divine nature'. He trusted this promise. That evening he reluctantly attended a Christian meeting in Aldersgate, London. There he felt his heart 'strangely warmed' and received an assurance of salvation, which set him off into an itinerant preaching ministry, covering 20,000 miles a year. Almost everywhere he preached, lives were changed, such was his trust in the promise that God would use him.

Meeting Jesus is about hearing the truth that sets you free (John 8:32). Whereas Plato taught a philosophy in which truth was to be sought, Christianity presents truth as something we seek, and something—indeed, someone—who also seeks us. We have God's own promise that holy scripture contains the truth necessary for our salvation. When we sit and read the Bible or hear the Bible read and explained in worship, we are reminded that truth is something outside us that challenges us, not just something we think out for ourselves. This is expressed by Paul when he says that 'our sufficiency is of God' (2 Corinthians 3:5, KJV) and 'it is God who establishes us' (1:21, RSV), and when he speaks of the church as 'the pillar and bulwark of the truth' (1 Timothy 3:15). God's truth sets us free, and it comes to us in Jesus through his instruments—the Bible and the Church.

Christians believe that the Bible cannot be mistaken as it presents the good news of Jesus to honest seekers of the truth. As the Bible says of itself in 2 Timothy 3:15, 'the sacred writings… are able to instruct you for salvation through faith in Christ Jesus'. This witness to God's salvation is the principal function of the Bible as a truth teller. Biblical truth is about relating one-to-one with God, in Jesus, first and foremost. Having said all this, many people's initial attempts to engage with the Bible are fruitless because they encounter it without repentance, thinking of it as less than it is—the word of God in human words. Moreover, like the Ethiopian court official whom St Philip enabled to understand the Bible in Acts 8, people very often need a human guide to help them get into scripture.

Former US President Theodore Roosevelt claimed that 'a thorough knowledge of the Bible is worth more than a college education'.[25] English Presbyterian clergyman John Flavel (1627–91) wrote that the scriptures teach us 'the best way of living, the noblest way of suffering, and the most comfortable way of dying'.[26] Do you want guidance on the use of money, on relationships, or on health of body, mind and spirit? It is all there in holy scripture. Do you want a vision for the purpose of history, or to renew your marriage, family or society? You can find help for these aims in the Bible, too.

We will always have questions about the Bible, but the Bible also has questions about us. Here's a final Bible-related quote from Mark Twain, who wrote with his typical humour, 'Most people are bothered by those passages in scripture which they cannot understand; but as for me, I always noticed that the passages in scripture which trouble me most are those I do understand.'[27]

Meditation

Open your ears to the word of God!
Read, mark, learn and inwardly digest holy scripture!
Let my word dwell in you richly!
The discernment of what is important
in the many demands upon you is to be found here.
Your own infinite value is affirmed;
the price of your salvation is stated.
Here can be found a purpose for living and a reason for dying.
I, Jesus, am God's Word made flesh
whose voice echoes down the centuries in the words of the Bible.
As you take in by faith what I have to say,
you will be drawn into eternal belonging with me
and your heart will be ignited with my holy fire.

(SEE MATTHEW 7:24–27; 24:35; COLOSSIANS 3:16)

In summary

Meeting Jesus takes us beyond reason into the realm of faith, opening the 'inner ear' to who he is and what he has done for us. This transformative experience challenges self-interest because Jesus died and rose so that we could die to self and rise to new life. This life is given us as 'rivers of living water' within (John 7:38) by the Holy Spirit. While it is given in baptism, it still needs releasing again and again because of all the issues in life that can act to quench it.

Friendship with Jesus draws us to his Father by his Spirit. The doctrine of the Trinity is nothing we could ever work out for ourselves. It is part of divine revelation, showing God to be love in himself, the love of Father and Son in the Holy Spirit who is their go-between. We simply cannot encounter Jesus without engaging with the triune God.

Jesus is the definitive Word of God who opens our ears to hear all that God promises us through scripture. This opening of our ears involves repentance and a readiness to let God have the final say over how we live our life.

For action

- Read through the Gospel of St Mark, the shortest of the four, to refresh your picture of Jesus Christ.
- Pray to God for more faith and, especially, for a vision of himself that is more to his dimensions and less to your own.
- Invite Jesus to meet you as you read a shorter letter of St Paul, such as Ephesians, Philippians or Colossians.
- Research the different daily Bible study notes available and consider trying a set, perhaps just for a month to start with.

CHAPTER 3

Open your eyes: The place of worship

'They came to Philip… and said to him, "Sir, we wish to see Jesus"' (John 12:21).

For 33 years, people could see Jesus if they could get to Judea and find him, although, in the last three years of his earthly ministry, they sometimes needed to go through his disciples. So we read in John's Gospel of a time when some Greeks were seeking Jesus: 'Philip went and told Andrew; then Andrew and Philip went and told Jesus. Jesus answered them, "The hour has come for the Son of Man to be glorified. Very truly, I tell you, unless a grain of wheat falls into the earth and dies, it remains just a single grain; but if it dies, it bears much fruit"' (John 12:22–24).

When Jesus is told that people want to see him, he speaks of his sacrifice, which is the very best he can offer them. When Jesus meets us, he calls us into worship, at the heart of which is sacrifice. Jesus died 'to gather into one the dispersed children of God' (John 11:52). He died and rose to gather us together into his sacrifice, entering into the movement of his self-offering to the Father.[28]

Christian worship is like an electric lift. It is not like a set of stairs that we have to climb in our own strength but, rather, like somewhere we place ourselves to be uplifted to the heavenly realm, the presence of God. Everything rests on entrusting ourselves, our souls and bodies, to Jesus who is the 'saving victim opening wide the gate of heaven to man below' in the words of the hymn by St Thomas Aquinas.[29]

To meet Jesus is to be drawn into worship, and to worship is to meet Jesus with his Father in the power of the Holy Spirit. Meeting Jesus in worship is also a corporate activity. You can never have Jesus to yourself, even though he has a very special love for you as an individual. The gathering of God's children into one worshipping body is the very mission of Jesus, who said, 'Where two or three are gathered in my name, I am there among them' (Matthew 18:20).

If we want our eyes opened to the worship of Jesus, we should turn to the last book of the Bible, called Revelation or the Apocalypse, which means an 'unveiling' of things to come. It contains glimpses of heavenly worship that centre on the sacrifice of Jesus:

After this I looked, and there was a great multitude that no one could count, from every nation, from all tribes and peoples and languages, standing before the throne and before the Lamb, robed in white, with palm branches in their hands. They cried out in a loud voice, saying 'Salvation belongs to our God who is seated on the throne, and to the Lamb!' And all the angels stood around the throne and around the elders and the four living creatures, and they fell on their faces before the throne and worshipped God, singing, 'Amen! Blessing and glory and wisdom and thanksgiving and honour and power and might be to our God for ever and ever! Amen.' (Revelation 7:9–12)

In this picture of heavenly worship, the multitude worships God and 'the Lamb', a sacrificial title for Jesus. As the lamb 'slain from the foundation of the world' (Revelation 13:8, KJV), Jesus draws the triumphant throng of the saints into the praise of God.

In this chapter, we continue to look at some of the ways people engage with Jesus Christ. Reason and faith put Jesus on the map. Prayer, Christian fellowship, service and witness are routes to deepening our relationship with him—but worship is central to engaging with Jesus.

The worship into which Jesus invites us was ongoing before the world was made and will continue when the world has crumbled to dust. Christian worship offered on earth is to be understood as the imperfect anticipation of the worship of heaven described in the verses from Revelation above. The Westminster Shorter Catechism sums up the purpose of human existence as 'to glorify God and to enjoy him forever'.[30] We are drawn more into that purpose as we soak ourselves in the worship offered day by day by the Christian Church. That worship invites the consecration of our life to God's praise and service.

Why worship?

I remember, when I became a student at Oxford University, visiting a number of city churches for Sunday worship. Once I had visited St Mary Magdalen's adjacent to Balliol College, my tour ended. There was something awesome there that drew my allegiance. The rich ceremonial was performed in an unself-conscious way. The parish priest, Fr John Hooper, preached not just about Jesus but as if in the presence of Jesus. The people were kneeling throughout most of the service and they seemed caught up into something awesome. I was intrigued, led along with them to meet Jesus in worship in a new way as I attended the traditional High Mass. In time I came to understand, through Fr John, that it was not something that so awed and fascinated me, but someone, the person of Jesus present in word and sacrament and fellowship, calling forth my allegiance.

I had found true worship. The Anglo-Saxon root of the word 'worship' means to give worth to something beyond ourselves. Worship is, to quote Evelyn Underhill, 'a devoted proclamation of the splendour, the wonder, and the beauty of God'.[31] To worship is to centre on God rather than self, even though we can never untangle the two. The Greek understanding of the word for worship implies submission to God; the Latin understanding is more intimate. *Adoratio* means, literally, mouth to mouth, the kiss of love. As we worship, we build a God-centredness in our life and in the community of faith that brings the holy influence mentioned earlier. As I discovered years ago in that Oxford church, there is something about the worship of Jesus that intrigues, reaching deep within and calling forth self-surrender.

We see this sort of worship anticipated throughout the Old Testament, especially in the vision of Isaiah:

In the year that King Uzziah died, I saw the Lord sitting on a throne, high and lofty; and the hem of his robe filled the temple. Seraphs were in attendance above him; each had six wings: with two they covered their faces, and with two they covered their feet, and with two they flew. And one called to another and said: 'Holy, holy, holy is the Lord of hosts; the whole earth is full of his glory.' The pivots on the thresholds shook at the voices of those who called, and the house filled with smoke. And I said: 'Woe is me! I am lost, for I am a man of unclean lips, and I live among a people of unclean lips; yet my eyes have seen the King, the Lord of hosts!' Then one of the seraphs flew to me, holding a live coal that had been taken from the altar with a pair of tongs. The seraph touched my mouth with it and said: 'Now that this has touched your lips, your guilt has departed and your sin is blotted out.' Then I heard the voice of the Lord saying, 'Whom shall I send, and who will go for us?' And I said, 'Here am I; send me!' (Isaiah 6:1–8)

Isaiah's vision of the thrice-holy God was so powerful that it reduced him to an abject surrender: 'Woe is me… a man of unclean lips.' This brought the redeeming gift of the live coal, blotting out his sin and drawing from him a new readiness to serve.

Parts of this passage are included in the central prayer of the Eucharist, because Christians see in these verses a statement of God's holiness, imparted to us in Jesus, the 'live coal', especially in the worship of Holy Communion. Unlike Isaiah, however, we are wise to the full personal revelation of God in Jesus Christ. When we look up in worship to God, we see him through the cross of Jesus. We see the love that gave itself for us and the holiness that demanded the offering because of our sin's affront to it. We see the Son of God who loved us and gave himself for us (compare Galatians 2:20).

Christianity is personal and purposeful. It is built around the one shown on Calvary to represent God's love for all and his purpose for all. The vision of God in the face of Jesus Christ both excites worship and fits us for worship.

See what love the Father has given us, that we should be called children of God; and that is what we are. The reason the world does not know us is that it did not know him. Beloved, we are God's children now; what we will be has not yet been revealed. What we do know is this: when he is revealed, we will be like him, for we will see him as he is. And all who have this hope in him purify themselves, just as he is pure. (1 John 3:1–3)

Meditation

Blessed be the God and Father
of our Lord Jesus Christ,
who has blessed us in Christ
with every spiritual blessing in the heavenly places,
just as he chose us in Christ before the foundation of the world
to be holy and blameless before him in love.
He destined us for adoption
as his children through Jesus Christ,
according to the good pleasure of his will,
to the praise of his glorious grace
that he freely bestowed on us in the Beloved.

EPHESIANS 1:3–6

Eye-opening sacraments

Worship is an eye-opener in Christianity because it is sacramental: that is to say, it employs signs that God, in Christ, has ordained to catch our attention. When Jesus died and rose, he passed into the sacraments. After his resurrection, he made himself known to his disciples through material signs such as breathing on them and breaking bread (John 20:22; 21:13). Jesus continues to use the elements of water, bread, wine, oil and human touch to convey his saving presence to his followers today. Through worship with 'outward and visible signs', God's 'inward and spiritual grace' is provided to us.[32] This divine love extends its ultimate embodiment in the flesh of Jesus down to all ages through the sacraments.

In a story told at the end of St Luke's Gospel, two disciples on the road to Emmaus after the resurrection encounter Jesus without recognising him. Their hearts 'burn' as he speaks to them from scripture (Luke 24:32). When they stop to eat together, he is revealed as Jesus when he breaks bread with them. The same invisible Lord continues to manifest himself in Christian worship through the sacrament of the Eucharist, which includes reflection upon scripture and the breaking of bread.

Jesus commanded us to plunge believers down into water in symbolic death (Romans 6:4). In the sacrament of baptism, the dying and rising of Jesus are branded upon us: 'As many of you as were baptised into Christ have clothed yourselves with Christ,' St Paul writes (Galatians 3:27). As Jesus died and rose, so Christians die and rise in this sacrament, which is best expressed for adults by the total immersion of the candidate. We go down to be buried with Christ; we come up to be clothed with him in his resurrection might. Through the water sign of baptism, we welcome Jesus who died in our place, showing our willingness for him to live in our place through his Spirit's descent into our hearts.

The five lesser sacraments similarly involve worship ceremonies in which people see aspects of God's love given to us in Jesus. These are known among Anglicans as confirmation, ordination, marriage, confession (the ministry of absolution) and anointing (the ministry of healing).

Confirmation has the sign of laying on of hands and anointing by a bishop, by means of which God gives strength by the Holy Spirit (see Isaiah 11:2; Acts 8:14–17). In ordination, there is the same sign of laying on of hands by a bishop, but with the expectation that God sets the candidate apart to be his sacred minister (see 2 Timothy 1:6; Titus 1:5–9).

The sign of marriage is found in the promises made by bride and groom to one another, through which God brings together a man and a woman for the rest of their lives (Mark 10:9). Confession (or the ministry of absolution) involves this sign: words of God's forgiveness being recited with authority over a repentant sinner by a priest. Through this, God assures an individual of forgiveness (John 20:22–23), an assurance that can also come by prayer and trusting the promises of scripture.

In the sacrament of anointing, a sick person is touched with oil that has been blessed by the bishop for healing, with the expectation that God will heal as he sees fit (James 5: 13–15).

The sacramental principle is that, just as human love is expressed bodily, so God uses the stuff of the visible world in order to demonstrate his invisible love. This love is shown supremely in the death and resurrection of Jesus, who lives on with us to 'make himself known in the breaking of the bread' (Luke 24:35) and other sacraments by his Spirit.

God, in Christ, uses the actions of sacraments as worship in a similar way to how he uses the words of the Bible to speak to us. Without understanding and openness to the inspiration of the Holy Spirit, sacraments, like Bible reading, can remain empty rituals.

Meditation

The creation itself—
sky, stars, sea, land, trees, flowers,
animals, humans—all speak of my divinity.
Open your eyes to these outward signs,
and your inner eyes to my invisible beauty and purpose.
On Calvary you see Jesus crucified
and, again, more than that—
you see how much I love you!
As invisible God I promise to reveal myself
to your faith in the sacraments of my Church.
Bread, wine, oil, water and touch are my instruments.
Oh taste and see how lovely the Lord is!

(SEE PSALM 34:8; ISAIAH 6:3; ROMANS 5:6–11; 1 CORINTHIANS 11:26)

Sunday Eucharist

Like the disciples who met Jesus on the Emmaus road on the first Easter Sunday, today's Christians are invited to meet him each Sunday in the breaking of bread, since every Sunday is the memorial of his death and resurrection. Christians joyfully accept this discipline of Sunday obligation to worship because they believe that Jesus rose from the dead on this, the first day of the week. Especially on Sunday, the Lord's day, the risen Lord Jesus greets us through signs he has invested with his power:

The Lord Jesus on the night when he was betrayed took a loaf of bread, and when he had given thanks, he broke it and said, 'This is my body that is for you. Do this in remembrance of me.' In the same way he took the cup also, after supper, saying, 'This cup is the new covenant in my blood. Do this, as often as you drink it, in remembrance of me.' For as often as you eat this bread and drink the cup, you proclaim the Lord's death until he comes.
(1 Corinthians 11:23–26)

The Lord's people gather on the Lord's day in the Lord's house around the Lord's table. As Pope Benedict XVI has said, 'At the celebration of the Eucharist, we find ourselves in the "hour" of Jesus... Jesus' hour seeks to become our own hour and will indeed become so if we allow ourselves... to be drawn into that process of transformation that the Lord intends to bring about.'[33] The Sunday Eucharist is 'the hour of Jesus' in which we soak in his presence in word and sacrament, to be refreshed as his disciples.

Meeting Jesus in the Eucharist goes much further than the spiritual refuelling of believers, however. 'Proclaiming the Lord's death until he comes' has global and cosmic impact. The memorial sacrifice that is the Eucharist lifts participants into the worship that began with the angels before ever creation was, and will continue with the angels and 'the righteous made perfect' (Hebrews 12:23) into eternity. In what we could call 'the hour of Jesus', the Church's Eucharist, we see 'the lamb slain from the foundation of the world' (Revelation 13:8, KJV) and are lifted up into the consecration of all life to God's worship and service.

I remember a Belgian priest, heavily committed to the justice that Jesus speaks of in the Gospel, describing the impact that his church's liturgy had had on a couple of atheist visitors to Sunday Mass. The men were meeting up with their friend before joining in a large demonstration for peace. They arrived early and sat at the back of church. Afterwards they spoke of an enviable sense of freedom in the Christian celebration. Although they were not believers, they were intrigued by the spirit among the congregation as they marked the day of resurrection by active, joyful participation in the Sunday Eucharist.

At the apex of the Christian Eucharist are the words of Jesus, consecrating bread as his body, and wine as his blood. They are followed by the prayer of Jesus, the Lord's Prayer, which people pray together, pledging themselves to the cause of Jesus. When a congregation stands, sometimes with hands raised, to recite this ancient prayer, there is a most powerful statement of intent that could well have a powerful impact on any observer. 'Our Father, who art in heaven, hallowed be thy name; thy kingdom come, thy will be done...' Those latter three clauses of the Lord's Prayer are translated by Eugene Peterson as 'Reveal who you are. Set the world right; do what's best' (Matthew 6:9–10, THE MESSAGE). To stand close to Jesus, as when taking part in the Eucharist, calling for God to be revealed and the world to be set to rights, is an awesome experience that draws people into a global and cosmic cause. The remaining biddings for forgiveness, guidance and daily bread prepare the petitioner for Holy Communion, which is Jesus' provision for the stated task.

A liturgical prayer used at the Maundy Thursday service states that 'as often as we celebrate this memorial sacrifice, the work of our redemption is advanced'.[34] I have already described the sacraments as 'eye-opening', and meeting Jesus at the Eucharist is an eye-opening business, both in the proclamation of his death (1 Corinthians 11:26) and in the resolution to work for the peace and justice of his kingdom 'until he comes' and God is made all in all.

In the Eastern Orthodox Church, we find an emphasis on Jesus using the participation of the faithful in the Eucharist as a means of bringing the world into the condition that he wants it to be. As the Orthodox priest and author Alexander Schmemann expressed it:

When man stands before the throne of God, when he has fulfilled all that God has given him to fulfil, when all sins are forgiven, all joy restored, then there is nothing else for him to do but give thanks. Eucharist (thanksgiving) is the state of perfect man. Eucharist is the life of paradise. Eucharist is the only full and real response of man to God's creation, redemption and gift of heaven. But this perfect man who stands before God is Christ. In him alone all that God has given man was fulfilled and brought back to heaven. He alone is the perfect eucharistic being. He is the eucharist of the world. In and through this eucharist the whole creation becomes what it always was to be and yet failed to be.[35]

The Sunday Eucharist is, in one way, a simple act of worship; in another way it is an act of cosmic significance, as vast as the work of Jesus it recalls, vast in the vision of cosmic transformation that it sets forth, a cause that will outlast us all.

Meditation

I am with you always,
beyond natural sight
yet visible to the eye of faith.
In the sacraments I seek to embrace you
and gather you into my earthly body
for the praise and service of my Father.
As at Bethlehem I veiled myself in flesh,
so now I veil myself in bread and wine,
for faith's discernment.
Sacraments will cease at my return,
when faith gives way to sight.
Meanwhile I am your food and your drink,
your Lord and your God.

(SEE MATTHEW 1:23; 1 CORINTHIANS 10:17; 11:24)

Be reconciled

'When you are offering your gift at the altar, if you remember that
your brother or sister has something against you, leave your gift
there before the altar and go; first be reconciled to your brother or
sister, and then come and offer your gift.' (Matthew 5:23–24)

Ugandan Bishop Festo Kivengere was a great preacher of forgiveness. Forced to flee Uganda after having been harassed to
within an inch of his life by the dictator Idi Amin, in 1973

he was eventually able to forgive his persecutor. He went on to write a book with the provocative title *I Love Idi Amin.*[36] Bishop Festo once talked of having to set off to preach while in the midst of a row with his wife. He slammed the house door and set off for church praying, 'Lord Jesus, go with me.' 'You go to church,' the Lord seemed to say back to him. 'I am staying here with your wife.' The bishop obeyed the prompting of Jesus, spent time seeking his wife's forgiveness, and went on to preach a magnificent sermon.

Meeting Jesus is also about meeting ourselves in our frailty. This is recognised in the structure of acts of Christian worship which often begin with the confession of sin and prayer for forgiveness. In this way participants are freed, by taking responsibility for their failings and welcoming God's forgiveness, to offer themselves afresh to his praise and service. 'If you forgive the sins of any, they are forgiven them,' Jesus said to the apostles (John 20:23). For 20 centuries, this ministry of forgiveness, of freeing from sin, has continued in his Church, particularly through the ordained ministry.

Jesus died that we might be forgiven, but we have to receive that forgiveness. We have to seek it. Why? To deal with our sins, because they drag us down. How? As the letter of James tells us: 'Confess your sins to one another... so that you may be healed' (James 5:16).

We need healing from guilt, the feeling that our sins are not forgiven. We also need reaffirmation of our belonging to God's family, the Church, when we stray into sin. The ministry of forgiveness, the sacrament of confession or reconciliation, is a Bible-based sign in which individuals are given a 'welcome home' to God and his Church through the authority of the minister. This ministry complements the assurance of forgiveness which is given to all Christians through prayer and the promises of scripture.

People may ask why they need to go to a minister rather than directly to God. It is not a matter of either–or. When the lost son in Jesus' parable felt sorrow for his sins, he said, 'I will get up and go to my father, and I will say to him, "Father, I have sinned against heaven and before you"' (Luke 15:18). Imagine his coming home to a note on the table saying 'All is forgiven' rather than to the extraordinary embrace of his father described in the Gospel account! As St Luke tells it:

While he was still far off, his father saw him and was filled with compassion; he ran and put his arms around him and kissed him… The father said to his slaves, 'Quickly, bring out a robe— the best one—and put it on him; put a ring on his finger and sandals on his feet. And get the fatted calf and kill it, and let us eat and celebrate; for this son of mine was dead and is alive again; he was lost and is found!' (Luke 15:20, 22–24)

Sacramental confession helps many Christians to receive that embrace and, with it, the knowledge that when God says they are forgiven, they truly are forgiven. By confessing specific sins to their minister and receiving one-to-one welcome, they find God's welcome back to them as individuals.

Christians may disagree about the ways in which they can receive assurance of God's forgiveness, but they all agree that church members should make themselves accountable both to God and to their church. Some are happy to use the minister as an instrument of this accountability, while others see it as introducing a go-between that could subtract from Christ.

It is significant that Jesus gave authority for his disciples to pronounce absolution, on Easter Day itself. That authority, established by his triumph over death, empowers those who seek to rise above the natural desire for retribution, as has been evident in Christian involvement in bringing reconciliation through, for example, the South African Truth and Reconciliation Commission. Belief that even death has been shrunk to size by Jesus continues to inspire agents of reconciliation to bring forgiveness in the face of human atrocities.

Meditation

Bless the Lord, O my soul,
and all that is within me, bless his holy name.
Bless the Lord, O my soul,
and do not forget all his benefits—
who forgives all your iniquity
and heals all your diseases,
who redeems your life from the Pit,
who crowns you with steadfast love and mercy,
who satisfies you with good as long as you live
so that your youth is renewed like the eagle's…
As far as the east is from the west,
so far he removes our transgressions from us.
As a father has compassion for his children,
so the Lord has compassion for those who fear him.

PSALM 103:1–5, 12–13

Liturgical and charismatic worship

I have been brought up as a member of the Church of England. This means that liturgical worship is second nature to me. I love the daily round of Matins, Eucharist, Midday Office, Evensong and Compline with which committed Christians are engaged, whether in the sung forms familiar in cathedrals or the more low-key approach found in many parish churches. This round or work of worship, we call 'liturgy', from a Greek word that literally means 'the people's work'.

While some may assume that an ordered pattern of corporate worship day by day is stifling, my experience is that it is actually freeing. You are given a natural starting point for prayer as you read scriptural texts that are being used right across the church that same day, and as you take, bless and share bread and wine in obedience to Jesus.

Meeting Jesus in liturgy is a matter of expecting his presence in scripture and sacrament. As with any routine, enthusiasm comes and goes, and, with it, the vital expectancy of faith. Liturgical prayer, sacraments apart, has the advantage that anyone can do it themselves, and groups of people can easily arrange to say daily prayer, known as the Office, together. In this way, believers encourage one another in the work of prayer.

Reciting psalms is a major part of liturgy. Sometimes described as the Jewish hymn book, the Psalter contains 150 inspired texts that are used in synagogues as well as churches to this day. Many of them read as a dialogue between God and the psalmist, so that saying a psalm means entering a conversation with God that can echo in our hearts during a time of reflection afterwards. This conversation is also that of

Jesus, who is to Christians both God and man. He is in on both sides of the dialogue. The human side of the dialogue moves from joy and thanksgiving to penitence, sorrow and even anger. As the psalm is offered as the prayer of the universal church, even if the mood of the psalm does not happen to fit your current situation, it is possible to identify with prayers being offered in other parts of the world in joy or sorrow.

Having said all this, as well as being rooted and grounded in liturgy, I have discovered over the course of my Christian life a movement that complements liturgical worship—the charismatic movement. I well remember visiting, out of interest, a charismatic service at St Matthias Church in Leeds in the 1970s, the early days of this movement in the UK. As I came through the door, a late arrival, I heard a loud harmonious singing without intelligible words. My instinct was to fall to my knees, because I was hearing something awesome, quite out of this world. Such was my first experience of singing in tongues. What impressed me was that, unlike liturgical prayer, this worship had no evident human organisation but rose to a crescendo, flowed on for several minutes and then ceased reverently, producing a deep silence.

Speaking in tongues is one of a number of supernatural gifts or charisms (hence 'charismatic') such as healing, miracles, prophecy and so on, listed in 1 Corinthians 12 and elsewhere, which can be exercised in worship. In charismatic worship, people receive words of guidance, healings and reminders of God's love for them from the Holy Spirit, which can bear fruit in a closer relationship with Jesus.

By reputation, charismatic worship is noisy, but the essence of it is about receiving an encouraging touch or word or vision from the Holy Spirit, which very often takes place in the silences that punctuate free worship. Such silent reflection is also popular within liturgical worship today. In more recent liturgical worship books, there are silences recommended after reciting the Psalms and after the scripture readings. I rarely celebrate the Eucharist without a minute or two of silence after the scripture readings and homily, and also after Communion.

The freedom and liveliness of charismatic worship is, for many people, a 'shock treatment' that can help to make Jesus real. For others, it is a stumbling block because of their fear of being manipulated by those involved in leading. If liturgical worship can be caricatured as stultifying, charismatic worship can be seen as distracting, yet both forms of worship work to bring people close to Jesus, who said, 'God is spirit, and those who worship him must worship in spirit and truth' (John 4:24).

If we go too far down the route of comparing different forms of worship, we can end up resorting to a kind of 'feel-good' rating that is essentially alien to the Christian understanding of worship. Though we live in a 'bespoke' culture, in which people can choose to personalise everything from the set-up of their mobile phones to (in some circumstances) the sex of their children, worship is by definition 'unbespoke'. It is God-centred and not self-centred—even if its power to sustain is enhanced when those who worship enjoy themselves at the same time.

Our prayer should be that our worship pleases God before it pleases us. What we feel like during 'Jesus' hour' is, to a degree, immaterial compared with how our life-attitude of sacrificial service extends from that hour into the remaining hours of the week. It is arguable that the high point of worship is the moment when we leave the assembly—and the nature of our worship is shown in whether or not we leave more in step with Jesus, more ready to head wherever he wants us to go next.

Meditation

I, Jesus, order and invigorate all things.
Through my gift, the song of praise
uttered in the highest heaven
has been brought to earth,
to be sung in order and freedom
from hearts that welcome me.
I inhabit the praises of my people,
in union with the Holy Spirit,
seeking to extend and amplify
the praise of God.

(SEE PSALM 22:3; MATTHEW 11:25–27; ROMANS 8:15)

In summary

When we meet with Jesus in worship, we are drawn to God's praise with the community of faith. We receive the Holy Spirit and we give of ourselves. Worship submits our life in loving adoration to God as the be-all and end-all through all eternity, and our worship has a personal focus in Christianity because God has been given a human face in Jesus.

Jesus lived and died and rose again, and gave us the

sacraments so that his risen presence could be made known to people in all ages. Just as human love is expressed bodily, so God uses the material things of this world to demonstrate his invisible love and draw us deeper into worship.

Christians accept the Sunday obligation to worship, especially attending the Eucharist, because this is the day when Jesus rose from the dead. The memorial sacrifice of the Eucharist shows forth his death and advances his kingdom, drawing participants into the transforming work that Jesus is accomplishing in the world.

Meeting Jesus in worship is also about meeting and accepting ourselves in all our frailty. The forgiveness that Jesus won for us on the cross is freely available through the worship of the sacrament of reconciliation (confession), as well as through personal prayer.

Jesus meets his people in worship through both liturgical and charismatic forms, and we can engage with Jesus in worship through scripture, sacraments and the extraordinary gifts or charisms that are given by the Holy Spirit. What remains essential, however, is that the fruit of all our worship is evident in the way it helps us keep our lives in step with Jesus, day by day.

For action

- Re-read this chapter's meditations slowly and ask Jesus to speak to you through them about worship.
- Go to a Sunday sung Eucharist at a local church. Before you go, examine your heart and mind so that the opening act of confession rings true for you.

- Attend a cathedral or parish church sung or said Evensong. Identify the prayer of the psalms recited on that day with either your own aspirations or those of others you know who are in joy or sorrow, need or gratitude.
- Read 1 Corinthians 12—14, about the use of the gifts of the Spirit. Attend a service at a local charismatic church, staying open to the possibility that God might speak to you directly through the worship.

CHAPTER 4

Open your heart: The place of prayer

If the heart is traditionally considered to be the centre of our being, it fits as a subject here in the central chapter of this book. Before we look at meeting Jesus in prayer and its connection with the heart, I should point out a potential problem with what you are reading. As mentioned previously, *Meet Jesus* presents seven routes to engagement with Jesus, linked to reason, faith, worship, prayer, fellowship, service and witness. The problem with this approach is the separation it makes between ourselves and Jesus, for St Paul tells us, 'In him all things hold together' (Colossians 1:17b)—and that includes you and me.

We want to invite Jesus into our hearts in prayer, but he is already there! He made us—with the Father and the Spirit—and he holds us in life. Having given us life, which he also sustains, he wants to give us *his* life, which is eternal. All the world lives in and through the power of Jesus, but it makes a difference if we wake up to that knowledge and invite Jesus to play a part in our lives.

The philosopher-priest Teilhard de Chardin wrote of the 'Christification of the universe'. He saw the risen Christ as being inseparable from the energy that holds the world in being and moves it forward. Where human beings own Christ, he enlists them to work for his plan to unite all things with God, the be-all and end-all.[37] To meet Jesus and engage with him is to be caught up into a movement of universal transformation. We human beings exist through and in and for Jesus Christ, who is bringing humanity to fulfilment as the light of faith spreads across the globe.

The internet, with its global connecting of minds, is an image of what Jesus is doing in the linking up of human hearts with his own heart in the community of faith. The fiery heart of lava within the earth is another symbol of the fire in the heart of Jesus, waiting to ignite souls with his passion for world transformation: 'I came to bring fire to the earth, and how I wish it were already kindled!' (Luke 12:49).

When we think about meeting Jesus in prayer, we should remember that prayer is both the lifting of mind and heart to God and the descent of the mind and heart of God into us. This dual movement is possible because of who Jesus is—both God and a human being. One of the most beautiful expressions of what goes on in Christian prayer, itself written as a prayer, is found in Ephesians 3:14–19:

I bow my knees before the Father, from whom every family in heaven and on earth takes its name. I pray that, according to the riches of his glory, he may grant that you may be strengthened in your inner being with power through his Spirit, and that Christ may dwell in your hearts through faith, as you are being rooted and grounded in love. I pray that you may have the power to comprehend, with all the saints, what is the breadth and length and height and depth, and to know the love of Christ that surpasses knowledge, so that you may be filled with all the fullness of God.

Prayer is meeting Jesus, glimpsing something of his infinite love and letting him dwell more and more fully with us and within us. It is also about being caught up into the love of

Jesus and what his love is accomplishing around us, both locally and globally.

We all need to be told we are loved, and the good news of Jesus is news of love stronger than death—divine love. The 16th-century saint Teresa of Avila taught people to pray in this way: 'Imagine you see Jesus standing before you... He is looking at you... Notice him looking at you lovingly and humbly. Prayer comes as you notice he is looking at you lovingly and humbly.'[38]

Scripture confirms the truth of St Teresa's words—that God, in Christ, looks upon each one of us with a tremendous love, however sinful we may be. He hates our sin but he loves us more than we will ever know or understand (Ephesians 2:1–5). Meeting Jesus in prayer is entering into this reality, being reminded of it day by day, hour by hour. It is the reality both of love and of the many good things that are ours to own in Christ and share with others. In prayer we realise the indwelling of the Holy Spirit given to us through baptism into Christ; as Thomas Merton wrote, 'In prayer we discover what we already have. You start where you are and you deepen what you already have, and you realise that you are already there.'[39]

We will turn soon to look at four ways of meeting Jesus in prayer, but first, here are some practical points for anyone thinking about a rule of daily prayer.

One of the most important issues to do with our daily prayer is the time we give to it. Whatever we feel or do not feel when we are at prayer, it is the offering of five, ten, 15 or 30 minutes daily that is pivotal. Commit your chosen amount of time to God and keep to it daily. It is also important to offer Jesus what we might call 'prime time', when we are not too tired or preoccupied with other matters. As well as designating a time, it is also important to choose a place of quiet—comfortable but preferably not too comfortable. Sitting on a straight-backed chair can be helpful, with occasional kneeling, perhaps on a cushion.

Prayer is a lifting of heart and mind to God, and there are many different ways that Christians can use to achieve this 'lift-off'. Experience shows, however, that it really helps to have a basic structure as you start praying, in case you end up floundering around and wasting time that could be used in prayer.

- As mentioned above, choose a suitable time of day, place and duration of prayer (for example, 10–20 minutes), find an optional visual focus, such as a cross or candle, and decide what you want to use as the starting point for your prayer. This might be scripture reading, contemplative silence, self-examination or intercession.
- Start by settling your body, relaxing your limbs and taking a few deep breaths.
- Come into God's presence. Come in praise of his majesty. Come in penitence before his holiness. If there are concerns you cannot shake off, turn them into prayer. Ask the Holy Spirit to be with you. You may feel it right to ask for some particular grace to be given to you through the prayer, such as insight for a particular situation you are living through, the grace of forbearance or a closer relationship with him.
- Start attending to God by use of your chosen starting point for prayer (scripture reading, contemplative silence, self-examination or intercession). Whenever you feel a 'heart tug' in your prayer, a sense that something is important to you personally, stay with it for a while rather than feeling obliged to continue with your planned meditation. Do business with God.

- Conclude by praying for others, thanking God for any graces or insights given and making a closing act of dedication to God's service, such as this prayer of St Ignatius Loyola (1491–1556):

Take, Lord, and receive all my liberty, my memory, my understanding, my entire will—all that I have and possess. You have given it all to me. To you, Lord, I return it. Everything is yours; do with it what you will. Give me your love and your grace. That is enough for me.[40]

Praying from scripture

Meeting Jesus in prayer is about listening and speaking. Since scripture has a particular authority as 'the word of God', it is an obvious place to go to listen to Jesus. The very existence of scripture is evidence of spoken dialogue between human beings and God. To pray with scripture can be, quite simply, an entering into that conversation, as we have seen already with the use of psalms in corporate worship.

For many people, prayer from scripture is aided by a form of imaginative reflection that originates in the Spiritual Exercises of St Ignatius of Loyola.[41] So-called Ignatian meditation engages with scripture using the mind, the heart and, most especially, the imagination. One such approach, the *lectio divina* method of reading the Bible, has three elements involved:

- Reading the chosen scripture passage.
- Meditating upon the themes and images in the passage, using the imagination.

- Praying in response to the passage and one's own meditations upon it.

In the prayer exercise below, we are invited to meet Jesus through the story of blind Bartimaeus in Mark 10:46–52. Although it was written down by St Mark long ago, in his story of the life of Jesus, this passage can come alive as you invite the Holy Spirit to make Jesus real to you here and now through the use of your imagination with the text.

They came to Jericho. As Jesus and his disciples and a large crowd were leaving Jericho, Bartimaeus son of Timaeus, a blind beggar, was sitting by the roadside. (v. 46)

1. Imagine Jericho, a city situated on the way to Jerusalem for Jesus and his northern followers from Galilee, and imagine Jesus approaching the time of his suffering and death—his passion. Out of the 20 pages of Mark's Gospel, ten deal with his suffering, death and resurrection. Chapters 1—10 set the scene for chapters 11—16, and this passage is the last word before Jesus enters Jerusalem on Palm Sunday.
2. The large crowd were, no doubt, not just drawn to Jerusalem for the Passover feast but also drawn to travel with Jesus to Jerusalem. Despite the likely preoccupation of Jesus with his imminent death and, more immediately, the pressing in of the crowd around him, Jesus is open to recognise the Spirit drawing him to stop and give his entire attention to one needy person—Bartimaeus, son of Timaeus.
3. As Jesus met with Bartimaeus, so he is available to meet with you and me, today, by the Holy Spirit.

When he heard that it was Jesus of Nazareth, he began to shout out and say, 'Jesus, Son of David, have mercy on me!' Many sternly ordered him to be quiet, but he cried out even more loudly, 'Son of David, have mercy on me.' (vv. 47–48)

1. Bartimaeus was given a special gift of faith to recognise Jesus for who he was—the 'Son of David', the Messiah, the one promised in the Old Testament who Isaiah said would 'open the eyes of the blind'. Imagine yourself beside Bartimaeus, hearing the Lord pass by on the way to the cross, in your dull spiritual sight crying out for his illumination.

2. 'Have mercy on me.' Would that be your prayer before Jesus today? How many times we call out for mercy in church services! We call out with our lips—but the prayer of the lips has to become the prayer of the heart. Only when we admit our need for God deep down can he fill us deep down, however many times we pray with our lips.

3. We note the determination and persistence shown by Bartimaeus. Jesus is halted by this cry of need, from a man so determined to get what he knew in his heart that Jesus could give to him. Bartimaeus was not messing around with the Lord: he meant business. It takes courage to lay all our soiled cards on the table before him, yet Jesus has deep compassion. Our sins are but dust before him.

Jesus stood still and said, 'Call him here.' And they called the blind man, saying to him, 'Take heart; get up, he is calling you.' So throwing off his cloak, he sprang up and came to Jesus. Then Jesus said to him, 'What do you want me to do for you?' The blind man said to him, 'My teacher, let me see again.' Jesus said to him, 'Go;

your faith has made you well.' Immediately he regained his sight and followed him on the way. (vv. 49–52)

1. Notice the eagerness and openness in that action of throwing off the cloak. To meet Jesus at a deep level requires readiness to 'throw off the cloak'. Facing Jesus involves letting him into areas of our life that he knows full well, but still needs our permission to engage with. It is up to us, not him, to reveal ourselves, to 'throw off our cloak' (or take it off bit by bit) for the healing work of divine mercy.
2. Jesus said to Bartimaeus, 'What do you want me to do for you?' Why? With this testing question, Jesus might have been making a final check on whether Bartimaeus really wanted to lose his blindness—which was, after all, a source of income. If he wanted to be healed, he had to be prepared to face the consequences and begin to earn his own keep rather than begging.
3. The fact that Bartimaeus followed Jesus shows that his cure was not just about physical healing but about a deeper work. His inner eyes were opened to the reality of God in Jesus, just as his outer eyes were opened to the world around him in all its beauty. Bartimaeus gained access to a greater beauty than physical sight can show us—the beauty of Jesus in his fullness as Lord and Saviour.

Meditation

Lord Jesus, we believe you are here
as you were in Jericho long ago.
We want to come into your presence, like Bartimaeus did.
We are casting off our cloaks now before you.
Touch our inner eyes, that we may see things as they really are.
Open our eyes to the reality of your presence with us
and our need of your mercy.
Make us ready to follow you as you summon us to go with you.
Jesus, bringer of sight and light, have mercy upon us
in your great compassion!

Prayer of contemplation

Meeting with Jesus in prayer is an extraordinary business, relating as we do to someone invisible, whose span is the universe and yet, at the same time, is the same as us in his human sympathies.

Just as there is a balance in love between giving and taking, so we may sometimes speak a lot in our prayers but then find out that our words falter—and then it is over to Jesus. As we sit in silence before the Lord, we hear his invitation to those first disciples in Gethsemane: 'Sit here while I pray' (Matthew 26:36). In the praying that is silent contemplation, there is a sense in which we sit and Jesus prays with us and in us, as we empty ourselves to be still and silent before him.

St John Vianney (1786–1859), otherwise known as the Curé d'Ars, excellent priest that he was, was drawn to prayerful parishioners. Fascinated by one farmhand's long sittings in church, he asked the man to explain what he was doing during those times. 'I look at him and he looks at me,' was the famous reply. There is no need for words when there is that sort of love.

What we do with silence, or how we cope with it, is very telling. To those who have faith in Jesus, silence is a fullness, an awareness of holy presence, at the heart of which we find God—Father, Son and Holy Spirit. As the psalmist wrote, 'Be still, and know that I am God' (Psalm 46:10).

There are many different kinds of silence, as we all know. To be silent with someone is actually quite an achievement in relationship. After many years of marriage, husbands and wives are often able to be in easy silence with one another and are happy to be so. At other times, silence seems to depersonalise us—for example, in a queue at a bus stop, where British social convention, perhaps over-concerned for personal security, makes for silence.

Silence before God is not depersonalising. Remember the words of the farmhand to the priest: 'I look at him and he looks at me.' We are caught up with Jesus into the relationship which is God, the three in one. As we empty ourselves before him, our whole being is drawn into his own prayer to the Father in the Holy Spirit, in which he gives glory to the Father from all eternity. And it is through the greatest of earthly prayers, the eucharistic prayer, that we are lifted up to enter into his self-offering, 'through Christ, with Christ and in Christ, in the unity of the Holy Spirit'.

Silent, loving communion with Jesus is as basic to Christianity as the silent, loving embrace of a mother for her child.

Yet although it may seem a wholly passive act, there is work to be done in contemplative prayer. It requires a conscious emptying of the mind and heart, or, to put it another way, a stilling of the mind in the heart, to be one with Jesus. For many of us, symbols (an icon, cross or candle) can help us to still our minds. Some Christians are helped in their contemplation by praying before the sacrament reserved in church for communion of the housebound. This can be a reminder of the Lord's presence, as the light that burns nearby indicates. Such contemplation is a recalling of the act of receiving Holy Communion, strengthening inward appropriation of Christ and the ability to see Jesus in friend and stranger.

The Roman Catholic writer and broadcaster, Bishop Fulton Sheen, described contemplating Jesus in the blessed sacrament as a form of spiritual radiotherapy. Just as we treat a cancer by exposing it to silent radiotherapy, so the soul is called to expose itself in silence to the physical presence of Jesus, with great potential for healing and cleansing.

Meditation

Be silent.
Be still.
Alone, empty before your God.
Say nothing.
Ask nothing.
Be silent.
Be still.

Let your God look upon you—
that is all.
He knows.
He understands.
He loves you with an enormous love.
He only wants to
look upon you
with his love.
Quiet, still be.
Let your God— love you.

ANON

Prayer of self-examination

Meeting Jesus in prayer as individuals complements our meeting with him for corporate worship. If we miss corporate worship, our personal prayer can become dimmed. Take away individual devotion, and corporate prayer can become ritualistic. This is why prayerful self-examination is so important. The apostle Paul, speaking to the Corinthians, calls them to make a special effort of self-examination before the Eucharist. 'Examine yourselves,' he says, 'and only then eat of the bread and drink of the cup' (1 Corinthians 11:28).

For Christians, prayer cannot be separated from right belief, celebration and action. Prayer is itself energised from right belief, from worship and from active love towards the world. This is set out by Jesus in the Lord's Prayer, which sets prayer within an overall aspiration for God's kingdom to come upon the earth. If the will of God were not frustrated by humankind's sinful choices, made through our free will,

Jesus would not have invited us to pray and work for his kingdom to come. Nor would he, in the same Lord's Prayer, have encouraged us to examine ourselves and to seek God's forgiveness for the ways we frustrate his designs, whether intentionally or unintentionally.

C.S. Lewis said that the only necessary requirement for prayer is honesty: 'May it be the real I who speaks.'[42] Self-knowledge is as vital as the knowledge of Jesus, and it is arguable that knowledge of God and knowledge of self are two sides of one coin. Only God can give us self-knowledge, release us from sin's power and consecrate the talents that should be better used in his service. To attain self-knowledge means a certain coming to ourselves, without which our lives can be an empty show. Without such a reality check, it is hard to give Jesus or anyone else a life that we do not possess.

Prayer that seeks self-knowledge from God is a lifelong struggle. As Fr Raniero Cantalamessa puts it graphically, we are like divers looking for a pearl, the pearl of a 'humble and contrite heart'. As we dive, we experience a sort of Archimedes' principle of the soul. The deeper a diver thrusts himself under water, the greater the upthrust of the water he is diving into, which forces him back up again: 'Whoever tries to dive below the calm water of his self-illusion, to humble himself and learn his true self, experiences the even stronger thrust of his own pride that tends to lift him above himself, so that he may emerge and remain on the surface.' The prayer of self-examination challenges such pride. It asks, 'Are you and I content to stay "on the surface" so far as God and our self-knowledge goes—or are we are prepared to expose our hearts to the light of the Holy Spirit and dive deep?'[43]

Prayer is the bringing of the whole self to God—the negative (sins, fears, sickness, doubt and so on) and the positive (gifts, relationships, the practice of our faith and so on). Sometimes, examination of the conscience has over-emphasised the negatives of our life. Jesus died for our sins, yes, and we need to be mindful of our failings. Yet Scripture also says, 'You were bought with a price' (1 Corinthians 6:20)—*you*, not just your sins. God is interested in the whole of us, not just the bits that need cleaning up. He seeks the release into his service of the good things in our lives alongside a purification of all that weighs us down.

A positive route to deeper self-knowledge is the prayerful pondering of the fruit of the Holy Spirit in Galatians 5:22–23: 'The fruit of the Spirit is love, joy, peace, patience, kindness, generosity, faithfulness, gentleness, and self-control.' It is good to recognise what signs of love, joy, peace and so on are growing in our lives, with a view to allowing this growth to be watered by openness to God's grace. Forget the weeds; concentrate on the fruit that is growing! This is very much an exercise of affirmation.

In meeting Jesus, we form a relationship with the one who can guide us to full humanity. By prayer we can see where he is leading us through our daily lives. As the Jesuit priest Jean Pierre de Caussade put it, our welcoming of Jesus in Holy Communion focuses the day-by-day, hour-by-hour welcoming of the Lord in our circumstances. Jesus is as ready to meet us in the circumstances of our life as he is to meet us in bread and wine.[44] The sense of security that this can bring is rightly celebrated by the psalmist: 'For the righteous will never be moved; they will be remembered for ever. They are not afraid of evil tidings; their hearts are firm, secure in the Lord. Their hearts are steady, they will not be afraid; in the end they will look in triumph on their foes' (Psalm 112:6–8).

The prayer of self-examination is the prayer of one who

aspires to this inner security and gladness of heart. Failure to accept the guidance of God revealed to us even in the worst of life's circumstances, the most evil tidings, is a recipe for becoming worn out and eventually destroyed. St Paul echoed this truth when he wrote, 'Give thanks in all circumstances; for this is the will of God in Christ Jesus for you' (1 Thessalonians 5:18).

A form for weekly self-examination

1. First, consciously enter the Lord's presence and cast your mind back over the last week, giving thanks for all the gifts you have received. Some may be great things and some seemingly insignificant—but all are gifts especially for you.
2. Notice, as you think back over the days, how the Lord has been working in you. What has he been asking of you? What has he been showing you?
3. What have your moods been during the week? Notice what brought you closer to the Lord. What has been his call to you? How did you respond?
4. Staying with your feelings, is there something that the Lord is showing you in a new way, something you would rather not look at, or something that the Lord is gently calling you to change? How do you want to respond?
5. Take a few moments to talk to the Lord about what you have discovered in this time of prayer and about any actions you feel called to take as a result of the prayer.
6. Ask for guidance and help through the coming week.

Praying the Jesus Prayer

I have known about the Jesus Prayer throughout my Christian life, but it is only in recent years that it has taken hold of me. It is an Eastern Orthodox devotion in which you repeat continually some variant of 'Lord Jesus Christ, Son of God, have mercy upon me, a sinner.' It is said formally at set prayer times and also freely as part of the unceasing prayer invited by scripture.

The Jesus Prayer expresses the good news of Christianity. It affirms both the coming of the Saviour and our need for his salvation. Based on incidents in the life of our Lord, it combines Peter's act of faith in Jesus ('You are the Son of the living God': Matthew 16:16) with the cry of the tax collector, 'Have mercy upon me, a sinner' (Luke 18:13b, TNIV).

This prayer exalts the name that is above every name (Philippians 2:9). It is the experience of countless believers that you cannot prayerfully repeat the name of Jesus without in some way touching his person, God's person. It is a form of Eucharist without the bread and wine—although, in my own personal experience, it comes into its own as an extension of sacramental Communion. 'The name of Jesus, present in the human heart, communicates to it the power of deification shining through the heart; the light of the name of Jesus illuminates all the universe', in the words of Orthodox theologian Fr Sergius Bulgakov.[45]

The Jesus Prayer is thoroughly evangelical and also uncompromisingly catholic. In other words, to pray it is to centre upon the good news of Jesus with the faith and prayer of the Church through the ages. Through repetition of the holy name of Jesus, we come to our own 'gospel' (good news) encounter, as his name eventually comes to convey his close presence.

Notice, I say 'eventually'! I have been heartened as I have pressed on in prayer, guided by the advice of St John of Karpathos: 'Long labour in prayer and considerable time are needed for a man with a mind which never cools to acquire a new heaven of the heart where Christ dwells; as the Apostle says: know ye not your own selves, how that Jesus Christ is in you?' (2 Corinthians 13:5).[46]

As someone whose mind is far from cool most of the time, I have found such advice most heartening. In the words of St Gregory of Sinai, 'Call to our Lord Jesus, often and patiently, and thoughts will retreat, for they cannot bear the warmth of the heart produced by prayer, and flee as if scorched by fire.'[47]

The Jesus Prayer is not primarily a cerebral activity but something that warms the heart as it helps us to embrace, however haltingly, the heart of God. The Orthodox anthology *Philokalia*, drawing on advice and insights from saints down the centuries, is concerned with helping the mind to become immersed in the heart in a way that resonates with the contemporary experience of baptism in the Holy Spirit. 'Abide constantly with the name of our Lord Jesus, so that the heart swallows the Lord and the Lord the heart and the two become one,' St John Chrysostom advises, going on to warn that 'this work is not done in one or two days; it needs long effort and a long time. For much labour and time are needed before the enemy is cast out and Christ comes to dwell in us.'[48]

In the past, one of the main obstacles to my adopting this form of prayer was the fear of consigning my prayer life to rote repetition. In fact, I have discovered that the reverent repetition of the Jesus Prayer actually brings with it the momentum of the Holy Spirit. This is brought out vividly in the beautiful story in the Russian Orthodox classic *The Way of a Pilgrim*, where the pilgrim learns to repeat the Jesus Prayer and eventually finds that it continues to be uttered deep within him, in the sense of Song of Songs 5:2: 'I slept, but my heart was awake.'[49] The phenomenon resembles speaking in tongues: it is an inner, gracious dynamic, 'for we do not know how to pray as we ought, but that very Spirit intercedes' (Romans 8:26).

How do we pray the Jesus Prayer? The traditional advice for formal use is to stand with eyes closed, focus upon the Lord and, after invoking the Holy Spirit, to repeat the phrase, 'Lord Jesus Christ, Son of God, have mercy upon me, a sinner', pausing briefly between each repetition.[50] A hundred prayers can be said in anything from ten minutes to half an hour, but those skilled in such prayer recommend that it should be neither gabbled nor offered in too intense a manner. To help focus the body's engagement in the exercise, prayer ropes with 25, 50 or 100 woollen beads are available (see www.cswg.org.uk for the contact details of one supplier). Carried in a pocket, prayer ropes can also be a good reminder to engage freely in the prayer during the day, especially as, unlike Western rosary beads, they do not rattle. I use such a 'Jesus rope' to get me going first thing, as part of my morning prayer, when I say a hundred prayers while standing. After my formal prayer time, I go on with the prayer as best I can, occasionally checking that my mind in repose is gently repeating the prayer.

As we focus on Jesus in this prayer, we can imagine the Holy Spirit descending upon him within us and also being part of his submission to the Spirit's work.[51] Another helpful way of using the Jesus Prayer is to build on and extend our last receiving of Holy Communion. linking the presence of

Jesus' name in the heart to the physical consuming of his body and blood in the eucharistic food. Yet another approach is to see our prayer as making ourselves part of the high priestly intercession of Jesus, again in harmony with the Eucharist. Even if the prayer is traditionally in the singular ('have mercy on me'), it is through Jesus who 'sustains all things by his powerful word' (Hebrews 1:3). Hence it brings with it the aspirations of the whole world. This sense of unity is echoed in *The Way of a Pilgrim*: 'I prayed with my heart, everything around me seemed delightful and marvellous. The trees, the grass, the birds, the earth, the air, the light seemed to be telling me that they existed for man's sake, that they witnessed to the love of God that all things prayed to God and sang his praise.'[52]

A last encouraging quote from the Orthodox *Philokalia*, the most famous anthology on prayer,[53] captures something of the positive, joyful goodness that flows from this discipline, even if such graces are inevitably sporadic: 'The sun, passing over the earth, produces daylight; the holy and worshipful name of the Lord Jesus, constantly shining in the mind, produces a measureless number of sun-like thoughts' (Hesychius of Jerusalem).

In summary

Prayer is a heart-to-heart meeting with Jesus, seeing his love and letting him dwell more and more with us and within us. It is being caught up into his love and helping to move forward what that love is accomplishing in the world. This is why the length of time we devote to prayer day by day is so important. Unless we have a set place and a basic structure, we can end up floundering around instead of entering God's presence.

Praying with scripture is always helpful and can be enriched by use of the imagination, as in the Spiritual Exercises of St Ignatius Loyola. Attaining silence, both outside and inside of us, is a vital aid to the discipline that is contemplative prayer, which can be focused on an icon, cross, candle or the blessed sacrament.

The prayer of self-examination roots our relationship with God in Christ in our personal circumstances, including our regrets, longings and aspirations. It can be served by using a structured form of conscience examination.

Finally, scripture invites unceasing prayer. An aid to the practice is the Eastern Orthodox Jesus Prayer: 'Lord Jesus Christ, Son of God, have mercy on me, a sinner', focusing as it does on the loving mercy of Jesus and the world's desperate need for him.

For action
- Try using the suggested structure for prayer every day for a week.
- Choose another healing story from the Gospels and develop a meditation along the lines detailed for the Bartimaeus story.
- Go in search of a silent place and read through the 'Be silent. Be still' meditation slowly and attentively.
- Try the suggested weekly self-examination exercise after putting faith in the presence of Jesus and his readiness to meet with you.

CHAPTER 5

Open your lips: The place of fellowship

A family I know were on holiday on a Greek island. They were having a meal in the local taverna when they were greeted by a friendly local. '*Koinonia*,' said the gentleman, waving his arms around the family circle to indicate their evident sense of belonging.

One of the great connecting words in the New Testament is this word *koinonia*, used in the original Greek text of these verses from Acts and translated as 'communion' or 'fellowship': 'They devoted themselves to the apostles' teaching and fellowship, to the breaking of bread and the prayers' (Acts 2:42–44). The first of Jesus' followers to meet with him after his death and resurrection had a fellowship with him that extended outward to fellow believers. Their commitment was to a body, the body of Christ, a fellowship built on teaching, sacrament and prayer, from which the Church developed as we know it, built on the same essentials.

The Greek word *koinonia* is used elsewhere in the early Christian writings of the New Testament to speak of communion with both God in Christ and fellow believers. The first letter of St John starts by speaking of Jesus, the need to proclaim him and the consequent *koinonia*:

We declare to you what was from the beginning, what we have heard, what we have seen with our eyes, what we have looked at and touched with our hands, concerning the word of life—this life

was revealed, and we have seen it and testify to it, and declare
to you the eternal life that was with the Father and was revealed
to us—we declare to you what we have seen and heard so that
you also may have fellowship [koinonia] with us; and truly our
fellowship [koinonia] is with the Father and with his Son Jesus
Christ. (1 John 1:1–3)

When someone says that they are a Christian, they will speak
of their *koinonia* with God in Christ, in the sense that they
know God personally through fellowship with Jesus. They
should also be willing to have *koinonia* with fellow believers in
subscribing to the faith and worship of the Church, because
meeting Jesus calls for a public commitment. As St Matthew
records, Jesus said, 'Everyone therefore who acknowledges
me before others, I also will acknowledge before my Father in
heaven' (Matthew 10:32).

For more than a few people, one of the hardest things
to accept about being a Christian and meeting Jesus is the
obligation to church membership. This is brought out vividly
in *The Screwtape Letters* by C.S. Lewis, which imagines the
correspondence between a senior and a junior devil:

I note with grave displeasure that your patient has become a
Christian. There is no need to despair; hundreds of these adult
converts have been reclaimed… One of our greatest allies is the
Church itself. Do not misunderstand me. I do not mean the Church
as we see her spread out through all time and space and rooted in
eternity, terrible as an army with banners. That, I confess, is a
spectacle which makes our boldest tempters uneasy. But fortunately
it is quite invisible to these humans. All your patients see is the
half-finished, sham Gothic erection on the new building estate…
when a patient goes inside… he sees just that selection of his
neighbours whom he has hitherto avoided… provided that they

sing out of tune, or have boots that squeak... or odd clothes, the
patient will quite easily believe that their religion must therefore be
somehow ridiculous.[54]

If only people could see Jesus' body—the Church—as God
sees her, as she really is, gloriously spread out through all time
and space and rooted in eternity, rather than as a handful
of curious-looking people with boots that squeak and odd
clothes!

Paul writes of the inadequacies of the church in a more
positive way: 'Christ loved the church and gave himself up
for her, in order to make her holy by cleansing her with the
washing of water by the word, so as to present the church to
himself in splendour, without a spot or wrinkle or anything of
the kind—yes, so that she may be holy and without blemish'
(Ephesians 5:25–27). The spots and wrinkles are certainly
there in the *koinonia* of the church, but they are on the way
out. This is the good news of salvation that Jesus is all about.

The communion of the Church

Even if the Church admittedly falls short of the example of
Jesus and gets in his way at times, it is still a fact that Jesus
founded the Church and promised to make her an instrument of communion with him, through his gifts of the word
of God and the sacraments (Matthew 16:18; 28:19–20;
Luke 22:19).

According to Article 19 of the Church of England Thirty
Nine Articles, 'The visible Church of Christ is a congregation
of faithful men [sic], in the which the pure Word of God is
preached, and the Sacraments be duly ministered according

to Christ's ordinance.'[55] To keep in touch with Jesus, we need both preaching and sacraments, and these we cannot, as a rule, get at home. The church is a fellowship united in 'the grace of the Lord Jesus Christ, the love of God, and the communion [*koinonia*] of the Holy Spirit' (2 Corinthians 13:13). To become a member, we need to be baptised with water 'in the name of the Father, and of the Son, and of the Holy Spirit'. At the font or baptistery, Christians are baptised into a union with Jesus and one another, including those believers who have already passed through death, in the common profession of Christian faith.

If baptism is the sacrament that brings us communion with Jesus in his Church, the Eucharist is the sacrament that brings that unity to full expression. The complete rite of Christian initiation involves preparation involving the deepening of repentance and building of faith, over months or years, leading to baptism and first communion at the Eucharist. Where a candidate has been baptised as an infant, the sacrament of confirmation precedes first communion.

Another important Greek word in Christian tradition, that encapsulates this formation of Christians, is *catechesis*. Summaries of Christian doctrine are often still called 'catechisms', initiation teachers are called 'catechists' and candidates are traditionally known as the 'catechumenate'. The word *catechesis* means literally to 'sound' teaching 'down into the ears'. Such teaching is voluntary and necessary as new Christians lay hold of the faith of the Church through the ages, expressed in the Apostles' Creed, sacraments, Ten Commandments and disciplines of prayer centring on the Lord's Prayer (See Appendix). *Catechesis*, or Christian teaching, is something that goes on beyond initiation and is essential to the collaboration or *koinonia* of Christians in the body of Christ, since such fellowship is built around obedience to 'the faith that was once for all entrusted to the saints' (Jude 3).

Receiving Holy Communion in the body and blood of Jesus is a gift that seals Christian unity. Those who share the sacrament in one place and time are one with those who share it in all times and places. Full Christian initiation makes us one with a body that is no less than an instrument of cosmic reconciliation. The 1982 Lima agreement of the World Council of Churches puts it thus:

The Eucharistic celebration demands reconciliation and sharing amongst all those regarded as brothers and sisters in the one family of God... All kinds of injustice, racism, separation and lack of freedom are radically challenged when we share in the body and blood of Christ. Through the eucharist the all-renewing grace of God penetrates and restores human personality and dignity. The eucharist involves the believer in the central event of the world's history. As participants in the eucharist, therefore, we prove inconsistent if we are not actively participating in this ongoing restoration of the world's situation and the human condition. The eucharist shows us that our behaviour is inconsistent in face of the reconciling presence of God in human history; we are placed under continual judgement by the persistence of unjust relationships of all kinds in our society, the manifold divisions on account of human pride, material interest and power politics and, above all, the obstinacy of unjustifiable confessional opposition within the body of Christ.[56]

To meet Jesus in the fellowship of his Church is to meet such a global challenge. It also involves living impatiently with the brokenness of the Church's universal fellowship, for, without such impatience, which should be manifested as a profound commitment to ecumenism, a Christian community becomes sectarian.

Christians approach the disunity of the Church in broadly two ways. For some, the different denominations, different styles and even different theological beliefs in the Church are not in themselves division, they say, but a celebration of the rich diversity of church life. There is no 'one true church' but Christians are one in Jesus. For others, the visible Church is part of the gospel message, and so church unity is essential. Roman Catholic, Orthodox and some Anglican thinking say with St Paul that 'because there is one bread, we who are many are one body, for we all partake of the one bread' (1 Corinthians 10:17). Christian unity is when people are in communion, or literally can take Holy Communion, with the local bishop. This has uncomfortable implications, since Roman Catholics, Orthodox and some other churches do not welcome those of other Christian denominations to receive Communion at their Eucharists, since that would presume an agreement in the faith that is not yet attained.

The lack of communion between Christians, and the divisions of the Church, are a serious obstacle to Christian witness, as they seem to say that Christianity does not work in practice. This is why Jesus prayed for his future followers '… that they may all be one. As you, Father, are in me and I am in you, may they also be in us, so that the world may believe that you have sent me' (John 17:21). Even if the last century has seen an encouraging rapprochement between the churches, there is much work to be done in building the visible unity that Jesus seems to desire. The spiritual unity already present among Christians of all denominations, along with so many common traditions, is a hand-rail that serves the ascent towards visible unity, which is also God's gift to be sought through united prayer.

Meditation

Just as surely
as unity dwells in my Godhead
and is the joy of my saints in heaven,
it is my desire for the church on earth.
Each year you celebrate my death on different days.
Each week you gather around different altars
to celebrate the sacrament of unity I gave you!
How can I reach an unbelieving world
through a body so disunited?
How can denominations
spring up almost daily in my name?
I, Jesus, am one—but you have divided me.
Look up to me, above your pride and rigidity,
and allow me to lay low the barriers
that crucify my body afresh.

(SEE JOHN 17:20–23; 1 CORINTHIANS 10:17; 11:27–30; 1 JOHN 3:11–22)

Where does authority lie in Christianity?

The faith of Christians is sustained within a body formed and authorised by God. This means that Christians exist in a community promised authoritative guidance in its task of bringing the whole world to the praise and service of God. As St Paul writes, 'Just as the body is one and has many members, and all the members of the body, though many, are one body, so it is with Christ. For in the one Spirit we were all baptised into one body' (1 Corinthians 12:12–13).

Where is authority in Christianity? It lies in the whole body of Christians and their agreement in faith, assisted by 'the Spirit of truth' who guides 'into all the truth' (John 16:13a) and by the promise of Christ that 'the gates of Hades will not prevail against [his church]' (Matthew 16:18b).

The very first church council authorised what 'seemed good to the Holy Spirit and to [the apostles and elders]' (Acts 15:28). The same apostles and elders had received authority from their Lord after his resurrection: 'As the Father has sent me, so I send you... Receive the Holy Spirit. If you forgive the sins of any, they are forgiven' (John 20:21–23). In the course of time, a threefold order of bishops, priests and deacons came to serve the essential ministries of preaching, teaching, pastoral care and celebration of the sacraments. To this day, ordained ministers carry authority to articulate the faith of the Church as a whole from one generation to another.

Authority in Christianity lies also with individual Christians, as, for example, in Christ's authorisation of individual believers to pray, witness, heal and deliver from evil. Whenever there is a disputed issue of faith or order, it is the building up of a common view, or consensus, from individuals in dialogue under the leadership of the ordained, that leads to an authoritative settlement.

The scriptures, creeds and decisions of the early church councils, such as Nicaea (AD325) upholding the Trinity, and Ephesus (AD431) and Chalcedon (AD451) affirming the two natures of Christ, human and divine, are recognised across major denominations as the bottom line for Christian teaching. Having said that, different parts of the Church give different degrees of authority to the Bible, to Christian tradition, to bishops or popes and to inspired reasoning. Within Evangelical churches, scripture is held as the supreme authority, sometimes interpreted literally. In Eastern Orthodoxy, the historic church liturgy, part of their worship tradition, holds particular authority. Among Roman Catholics, the Pope, as successor of St Peter, is held to possess a special gift when he acts with Catholic bishops to formulate the truth of Christian revelation. Among Anglicans, scripture, tradition and inspired reason have been described as the 'three-legged stool' upon which all teaching rests.

Different parts of the Church also differ on the relationship between the authority of conscience and the teaching authority of the Church. Interestingly, when Cardinal Newman said that he would drink to the Pope but to conscience first, he affirmed the authority of any conscience formed by Christian teaching. Christianity struggles to effect such formation today across all the branches of the Church. Ideally, moral teaching is presented to individuals with an authority that is clear on principle and yet, at the same time, caring towards them and their own struggles. A pastoral approach, which seeks to challenge those who need challenging without discouraging those who struggle, is a vital part of promoting allegiance to authoritative teaching. This is the genius of Jesus himself, who persuaded so many to follow his way because he 'taught them as one having authority' (Matthew 7:29) while still showing compassion. For example, although he affirmed faithfulness in marriage, he had gracious dealings with people who had fallen short of that ideal (see John 4:16–26; 7:53—8:11).

In recent years, a number of ethical issues have proved a severe test of authority to the churches. There has been polarisation between traditionalists and revisionists on issues such as contraception, women's ordination and same-sex relationships. These debates have challenged those in authority within the churches to be both courageously countercultural and prudent, discerning what the Spirit may be saying through Christian experience on issues of the day. The different cultures of the world challenge authoritative church teaching from different directions, which makes the recovery of universal Christian agreement in the faith all the more important.

Of course, in Christianity, ultimate authority comes from God through the Church. Although Christians divide on some questions, they agree on the need to welcome this gift of authority from God as his provision to keep his Church on track in the mission he has given her. Misuse of authority in the Church over the centuries has served to multiply Christian divisions. As Christians recover a fuller agreement in faith, a servant-hearted (not heavy-handed) exercise of authority appears to be the best way of helping to build more agreement for the future.

Meditation

All authority in heaven and on earth
has been given to me.
Go therefore and make disciples of all nations,
baptising them in the name of the Father
and of the Son and of the Holy Spirit,

and teaching them to obey
everything that I have commanded you.
And remember, I [Jesus] am with you always,
to the end of the age.

MATTHEW 28:18–20

The challenge of relativism

Two centuries ago in England, the great majority of people accepted the Church of England, with a small proportion of dissenters. Today's electronically connected world is such that English people question the formerly authoritative truth of Christianity itself, let alone that of the Church of England. People are looking to different authorities for truth. It is as if everyone is a dissenter, as if everyone has got to find their own personal authority.

'Christianity might be true for you but it's not true for me. We all need to make our own way in life.' This is a very attractive philosophy today, sometimes called 'relativism'. It sees all truth claims as linked to the individual's subjective taste, so that all truth is relative and never absolute. Why, indeed, should anyone impose truth on anyone else? Truth should commend itself. The modern world is modern because people have had the courage to bring hallowed traditions and truths into question. Sometimes modernisation brings good; sometimes, though, it brings a demoralising confusion.

Jesus himself taught truth by telling stories, and went on to put his life on the line for what he taught. Nevertheless, he respected dissenters from his truth, like the rich young man who went away from him 'grieving, for he had many possessions' (Mark 10:22). Truth can hurt, yet Jesus did not run after the young man. Many a time in the Gospels, we see Jesus entering dialogue with people but leaving them with open questions.

Too often throughout history, the Church has forced 'the truth that is in Jesus' (Ephesians 4:21, NIV) upon people in a way that Jesus would never have entertained. It should be no surprise to us that formerly so-called Christian cultures are now rejecting that sort of imposition. It is not that the truth found in Jesus about life and sex and money and power has changed. It is just that people have been distracted from that truth, not only by the world around them but, sadly, by the falling short of very many followers of Christ through the ages. The consequence of this distraction is the increasing prevalence of views such as 'Christianity's not true for me' and 'We can all find our own path to God.' I think it is sad that people feel forced to make their own way to God when God has made his own way for them to follow in Jesus. Can we blame God if too many of those who follow that way fall short?

In becoming Christians, people move from asking questions of the Christian Church (dialogue) to being asked questions themselves by the Church (*catechesis*). As they grow in faith, they develop a growing acceptance of the authority of Jesus Christ exercised through his Church, and a desire to be formed in the apostolic faith 'uniquely revealed in the Holy Scriptures and set forth in the catholic creeds, which faith the Church is called upon to proclaim afresh in each generation'.[57]

There is little doubt that this confidence of Christians in

what God has said and done can upset and offend people. Inevitably, at one time or another Christians find themselves accused of being arrogant, or of thinking they are always right. In the Bible, God speaks with certitude of Jesus Christ, that salvation is found in no one else, 'for there is no other name under heaven given among mortals by which we must be saved' (Acts 4:12). He who is truth lends authority to the Church of Jesus Christ as 'the church of the living God, the pillar and bulwark of the truth' (1 Timothy 3:15b).

The challenge in speaking out for Jesus in an age where truth is relative is to do so relationally—that is, with both love and confidence. Truth should commend itself. It does so in Jesus, especially through those who have recognised him for who he is and seek to be his loving witnesses. As we have already seen, the Christian view is that the truth is more than just something you and I perceive. It is something seeking us—the God who is truth. Jesus expressed it in parable form: 'Which one of you, having a hundred sheep and losing one of them, does not leave the ninety-nine in the wilderness and go after the one that is lost until he finds it? When he has found it, he lays it on his shoulders and rejoices' (Luke 15:4–5).

Meditation

I am
the Way for you to walk,
the Truth for you to tell,
the Life for you to live.

Though the world
puts faith in me alongside other creeds,
I stand above and beyond the world.
Those who put faith in me
will never be confounded
or cast down.
All time and eternity is mine
and in my presence is joy abounding
and perfect peace.

(SEE PSALMS 22:5; 34:5; JOHN 14:6; 1 PETER 2:6; REVELATION 1:8)

The challenge of hypocrisy

In May 2010, Pope Benedict XVI made headlines when he said, 'The greatest persecution of the church doesn't come from enemies on the outside but is born from the sins within the church.'[58]

'I believe in Jesus but the church is a load of hypocrisy.' This is an objection to Christianity that makes me sit up! I believe in Jesus too, but I do not always live up to the standards expected of his followers. Does that make me a hypocrite? The definition of a hypocrite is someone who pretends. I do not pretend that Jesus has the truth or that he is the truth—I know it—but I also have to admit that I fall short of him. When we meet Jesus, he gives us a vision. We try to live up to it, and inevitably we fail, but where would we be without that vision? Having his standards is like having your alarm clock set half an hour ahead to make sure you are never late. Similarly, in the Gospels, Jesus taught things that would keep us on our toes, pressing forward towards his perfect standard. Here are some examples from St Matthew's Gospel: 'Forgive your brother or sister from your heart' (18:35); 'Everyone who looks at a woman with lust has already committed adultery with her in his heart' (5:28); 'Do not worry about your life' (6:25). Which of us has not fallen short in at least one of these areas?

Thankfully, Jesus knew that his followers would fall short and he taught that, when it happened, we could ask for God's forgiveness. Every church service includes a time of repentance, for confessing our failings. In the Gospels we read how those who cheated others came to Jesus and were forgiven; those who had stolen, those who had sold their bodies for sex—all came to Jesus and were welcomed. Ephesians 2:4–5 says, 'God, who is rich in mercy, out of the great love with which he loved us even when we were dead through our trespasses, made us alive together with Christ— by grace you have been saved.' If someone tells me that they believe in Jesus but that Christians are hypocrites, I can tell them how the mercy of God covers my sins. I can tell them of the God and Father of Jesus, who loves sinners and gives them not what they most deserve but what they most need— the encouragement to get up and press on when we fail.

We have to do more than defend Christians, however. To answer fully the charge of hypocrisy, we need to defend the institutional Church. We cannot abandon it to its detractors. The Church may fall short of Jesus but it is also true that Christians need the Church. We read in Matthew 16:18 how Jesus founded the Church, saying, 'I will put together my church, a church so expansive with energy that not even the gates of hell will be able to keep it out' (THE MESSAGE).

We need that energy. If you believe in Jesus but ditch the Church, your belief will not go far. As previously mentioned, we know that the first believers 'devoted themselves to the apostles' teaching and fellowship, to the breaking of bread and the prayers' (Acts 2:42). The writer of Acts goes on to say how 'many wonders and signs' were evident in the church and how believers 'were of one heart and soul... and great grace was upon them all' (2:43; 4:32–33).

As a Christian, I want that grace! I want to come close to Jesus and receive it day by day. Whatever people say about hypocrisy in the church, I want to ask them how I can get close to Jesus better than through the church. Where else can I hear God's word expounded? Or encounter the Lord by praying with other believers? Or welcome the promised Holy Spirit? Where but in the fellowship of the Christian church can I receive the spiritual food of the precious body and blood of Jesus in Holy Communion?

A great evangelist had a fireside chat with a young man who insisted that it was possible to believe in Jesus without going to church. Having reminded him that faith in Jesus grows up in a community, the evangelist reached down for the tongs and took hold of a brightly burning coal, removing it from the heart of the fire. As he held it aloft, the two men saw it gradually change from red to orange to black. The young man was in church the next Sunday!

Even if there is hypocrisy in the church, Jesus is there also, among his people, waiting to warm their souls. As he said himself, 'Where two or three are gathered in my name, I am there among them' (Matthew 18:20).

Meditation

*Lord, your good news is easy to hear
but hard to act upon.
Those of us familiar with your good news
forget the shock of the invitation
to lose our life so we can gain it afresh in you.
We see an ocean of need around us
and question the difference we can make.
We recognise our mixed and lukewarm motivation
as followers of Jesus.*

*Take heart, my sisters and brothers!
I, Jesus, look less upon your failings
and more upon your aspiration
to be with me in setting the world right,
through loving with more of
your heart, soul and strength.*

(SEE MARK 12:28–34; JOHN 18:15–18; 21:15–19)

Think global—act local

When you meet Jesus, he draws you into his Father's never-ending family, the 'holy, catholic church'. The vision of the Church is immense, stretching back in time through 20 centuries and across the continents of the earth. To be in timeless fellowship with angels and saints in worship and prayer is a privilege associated with 'the freedom of the glory of the children of God' (Romans 8:21b).

The *koinonia* of Jesus' Church is both universal and local, and we forget either aspect at our peril. The universal vision is useless without a local incarnation. As already mentioned, the local Christian fellowship becomes sectarian unless it aspires through *catechesis* to the faith of the universal Church. Christians come to active faith through immersion in a local community that believes in Jesus. Our profession of faith is joined to that of others in our locality with whom we say the creed, share the sacraments, live the commandments and accept a discipline of prayer. As Californian worship leader and teacher Bridget Willard says, 'Church isn't where you meet. Church isn't a building. Church is what you do. Church is who you are. Church is the human outworking of the person of Jesus Christ. Let's not go to Church, let's be the Church.'[59]

This is the challenge of Jesus to anyone reading this book. To belong to Jesus Christ is to belong to a local branch of his 'human outworking'. Just as the universal Church was founded when Jesus was conceived in Mary at Nazareth, so its local branches grow up as the reality of Jesus impinges locally through prayer, preaching, teaching, sacraments and outreach. You cannot open your lips to own Jesus without committing yourself to stand alongside all those who do the same in your vicinity. Your own capacity to share about Jesus will be enhanced by evidence of his transformation in your life—and also in the lives of other members of your worshipping community.

In his book *The Provocative Church*, Graham Tomlin sets out the main priority of the Christian church locally as being to generate a community that intrigues because it gives a taste of the joy, generosity and deep sympathy of Jesus' coming kingdom. Just as an Irish bar in Kilburn gives Londoners a taste of distant Ireland, so the local church is a taster of the real thing—a memorable analogy![60]

Such a 'provocative' church intrigues because it is full of unfashionable mercy, creativity, love and humility. To achieve such a church requires a humble leadership, secure in Christ, who encourage a whole variety of ministries, all geared to the task of evangelism. While evangelism should not be prioritised apart from social commitment and spiritual renewal, it is vital for leaders to challenge individual believers to be more public about their Christianity, to build confidence about telling their faith stories, perhaps by meeting in cell groups, and to be ready to issue invitations to seekers. When we open our lips to name Jesus as Son of God and Saviour, we place ourselves alongside millions on the earth today. The difference our profession makes will largely depend on our finding common purpose in praise and service with fellow Christians in our locality. 'We have this hope, a sure and steadfast anchor of the soul' (Hebrews 6:19), and this faith is, as the metaphor implies, one that both stabilises the Christian community and makes it an attractive haven for all who are adrift in the tempests of earthly life.

Meditation

A new creation began as I came from a virgin womb
and was revealed in my proceeding alive
from the realm of the dead
and the powerful coming of the Holy Spirit.

I, Jesus, delight to make the impossible possible
as my people put faith in me and not just in human thinking.
The hope I bring is no sedative but a shot of adrenalin!
As my people seek me, they find me
as I come among them.
lending power and love
that excites and draws.

(SEE GENESIS 1:1; JOHN 1:14; ACTS 2:1–4, 43–47)

In summary

Meeting Jesus leads to public commitment. It involves willingness to have fellowship with fellow believers and subscribe to the faith and worship of the Church through the ages. People make a public commitment to Christ at baptism. They commit (or their godparents commit on their behalf) to the creed, sacraments, commandments and disciplines of prayer (see Appendix). Regular participation in the Eucharist holds them to that public commitment to Jesus and his body, the Church.

The faith of Christians is sustained within a body, the Church, formed and authorised by God. Through the scriptures, Christian tradition and the gift of the ordained ministry, Jesus lends authority to his Church to make disciples of all nations. We have an assurance that Jesus brings full salvation to all who turn to him, although this assurance often offends in a culture where truth claims are seen as subjective and relative.

People often accuse Christians of hypocrisy. The failure of all of us who profess Jesus yet do not live up to his standards is undeniable, but the good news of Jesus is about helping us to admit our need for improvement and to welcome the help he readily provides.

Local church membership relates to the universal Church and the faith it has held since the apostolic age. It also relates to our own local community and the challenge to work with fellow Christians around us to worship God and share the hope that Jesus brings to life.

For action

- Search out and read the statement of faith or cate-chism of a part of the Church with which you are less familiar.
- If you are a confirmed church member but you feel a bit rusty on what it all means, consider repeating confirmation classes to refresh your understanding.
- Research some of the positive achievements of the Church in terms of its impact on the world, to bal-ance out its well-documented failures. Take a look, for example, at the healing ministry or Christian work in the rehabilitation of prisoners.
- 'Church is what you do… let's not go to Church, let's be the Church' (Bridget Willard). Find a Christian community that seems to be making a positive im-pact in your neighbourhood and get involved in it.

CHAPTER 6

Open your hands: The place of service

You get to know people by working alongside them, and it is the same with Jesus. The very name of Jesus means 'saviour', reminding us of God's desire to set the world right, so sharing in the concerns of Jesus draws us into practical works of service. Jesus sees the 'big picture' of life and so he is able to expand both our minds and our hearts. To acknowledge the truth about the way the world is helps us begin to identify the best ways to get involved in making a difference.

A young man attended a church whose grounds were popular with vagrants. As he passed these people on his way to worship, Sunday by Sunday, they became part of his prayer in church. Eventually he felt that Jesus was asking him to raise interest in organising a regular lunch for them. The lunch came to involve not just the church members but many others in the community who had a concern for the poor.

When Jesus talked about God at work, he used images of small beginnings escalating towards powerful outcomes. He once said, 'What is the kingdom of God like? And to what should I compare it? It is like a mustard seed that someone took and sowed in the garden; it grew and became a tree, and the birds of the air made nests in its branches' (Luke 13:18–19).

Just as, in nature, a seed sprouts and grows with enormous consequence, so it is in the realm of salvation that Jesus opens up with his co-workers. Salvation is about people gaining

117

both materially and spiritually, as Jesus clearly demonstrated during his earthly ministry, helping those who trusted him to assist in making a difference to the lives of others. Even his most spectacular miracles involved the assistance of ordinary men and women. When faced with 5000 hungry people, Jesus borrowed bread and fish from a trusting boy and invited his disciples to hand it out to the crowd. Only as the disciples got on with serving the crowd did the food multiply and become sufficient to satisfy everyone's hunger (Matthew 14:13–21).

When we read the stories of Jesus in scripture, we pick up on his concern for the needy—a concern that continued to be characteristic of his disciples after the resurrection. Those disciples were told to love God and neighbour, to preach and to heal, to worship and to serve the poor. They were also promised specific guidance about how best to employ their energies in helping others.

'God is faithful; by him you were called into the fellowship of his Son, Jesus Christ our Lord,' wrote St Paul (1 Corinthians 1:9). When we meet Jesus, we are called into partnership with the community of faith in serving 'the kingdom of the world [which is becoming] the kingdom of our God and of his Christ' (Revelation 11:15). This service has the ultimate aim of bringing the life of God in Christ to bear upon all things—not only our own inner life but our community life and even the life of the cosmos.

By his coming on earth, living, dying and rising again, Jesus has brought remedies for all that pulls life apart. This good news is entrusted to his partners on earth today to flesh out in the attention and service they provide in their immediate locality day by day. We learn what to do as we go along with Jesus, and we learn from one who is expert in serving the best interests of human beings. This servant-calling is well expressed in the opening paragraph of the encyclical on the church in the modern world from the Second Vatican Council (1962–65): 'The joys and hopes, the griefs and the anxieties of the men [sic] of this age, especially those who are poor or in any way afflicted, these too are the joys and hopes, the griefs and anxieties of the followers of Christ.'[61]

Forgetting self

The choice to give our time and energy to serve other people is one that very often seems to go against self-interest. One Holy Week, a forceful nun persuaded me to celebrate the Eucharist in a residential home in a nearby parish. It really did seem to be beyond the call of duty that week, given the other demands on a priest engaged in organising Easter services. As no one else could be found, I went, rather reluctantly. Forty residents attended, many in wheelchairs. I administered Holy Communion, and I recall one of the elderly women having great difficulty receiving the sacrament, although she managed in the end with my help. That night, the nun phoned me to say that this woman's Communion had been the first food she had apparently eaten for a week. After the service, she went on to eat a light supper and then died peacefully.

I was glad that I had overcome my self-interest to bring that elderly woman a sacramental encounter with Jesus, putting her soul at rest so that she welcomed his ultimate call. Inevitably, the forceful nun then called on me to conduct the woman's funeral, but I found a new readiness to serve within me—and it was after Easter!

We cannot give what we do not possess. Readiness to serve flows from being in some way in control of our life. Sometimes when I visit churches I see faces with need written all over them, indicating that the available energies for service in that church will be limited. Where people are heavily self-preoccupied, they are not sufficiently able to rise above their own agendas to sympathise, let alone provide for others. At other times and in other places, I encounter people whose enthusiasm almost knocks me over. This can lead to the opposite problem—a determination to give out to others that does not sufficiently consider other people's perspectives or their natural reluctance to welcome assistance from anyone, which stems from a healthy independence.

One truth that Jesus teaches his followers is the importance of sitting lightly to self-interest. People who live close to God seem to gain a certain selflessness. This can come by osmosis, simply soaking in the Lord's presence, although deliberate acts of self-denial play their part in the shaping of the spirit that Jesus invites. Self-emptying is central to all that Jesus is about: 'For you know the generous act of our Lord Jesus Christ, that though he was rich, yet for your sakes he became poor, so that by his poverty you might become rich' (2 Corinthians 8:9).

In his autobiography, Christian writer and thinker Henri Nouwen tells of his spiritual journey, moving from an academic role as a professor at Harvard Divinity School to live among people with developmental disabilities at the L'Arche Daybreak Community in Canada. Nouwen describes his struggle with intellectual pride and the blessings he received as he countered his arrogance:

People seek glory by moving upward. God reveals his glory by moving downward. If we truly want to see the glory of God, we must move downward with Jesus. This is the deepest reason for living in solidarity with poor, oppressed and handicapped people. They are the ones through whom God's glory can manifest itself to us. They show us the way to God, the way to salvation... Yet everything in me wants to move upward. Downward mobility with Jesus goes radically against my inclinations, against the advice of the world surrounding me.[62]

If Jesus counters anything in us, it is the pride that counters the best use of our gifts. Nouwen's story is particular to him and his own perception of where he could best make a difference at a certain stage in his life. Nevertheless, we can all be deceived by pinnacles of achievement into a self-satisfaction that subtracts from the good we might further achieve if we could turn our eyes away from self.

Meditation

Let the same mind be in you that was in Christ Jesus,
who, though he was in the form of God,
did not regard equality with God
as something to be exploited,
but emptied himself,
taking the form of a slave,
being born in human likeness.

And being found in human form,
he humbled himself
and became obedient to the point of death—
even death on a cross.

PHILIPPIANS 2:5–8

Receiving to give

Years ago, I worked among the indigenous people of Guyana. In our location there was a lake in which we used to bathe, close to the Rupununi river. In the rainy season it was fresh, but, as the dry season extended, it became foul. The lake needed the river water to irrigate it by flowing in and out, but this flow ceased for part of the year and meant we had to walk a lot further to bathe.

The lake is a parable of service with Jesus. We go stagnant without the irrigation of his Spirit. We need to receive from him to keep enthusiasm in our faith. At the same time, just as a lake is in danger of stagnation if it has no outlet for releasing its water, so it is with a Christian life that lacks service.

Self-emptying is hard, but it is easier with Jesus alongside, since he is always wanting to lend us his strength to grow into his likeness. St Paul wrote about how he had come to see Jesus affecting his every circumstance in this fashion: 'I know what it is to have little, and I know what it is to have plenty. In any and all circumstances I have learned the secret of being well-fed and of going hungry, of having plenty and of being in need. I can do all things through him who strengthens me' (Philippians 4:12–13).

We open our hands to Jesus so that he can take us and use

our strengths to make a difference to the world, even through the particular circumstances of our daily lives. If our hands are clenched, they are combative and self-assertive, whereas when they are open they are ready for unselfish service and for receiving gifts to bring to others.

Many times I encounter a situation that angers me and makes me mentally clench my fists. I often come to realise that what is angering me is my hurt pride. I have to unclench those inner fists to say, 'Sorry, Lord; forgive my pride and take my hand in this situation.' By receiving from Jesus, I am able to give out love, joy and peace, which certainly would not have been the outcome unless I had repented and turned to him and his gracious provision.

Sometimes Jesus calls us to examine ourselves, to identify things inside us that block our receiving from him, so that we go on to seek the ministry of prayer and healing. When we have been hurt in the past, it damages the level of trust we bear towards others, so that we end up erecting protective barriers around ourselves. These may help us live our lives but they can affect our capacity to receive love and to give it out. We cannot always see these needs ourselves, and it is significant that when Jesus sends people out in the Gospel accounts, he sends them in pairs so that they can help one another in his service. This helpfulness is evident today in the ministries of forgiveness, healing and spiritual direction within the Church.

'I can do all things through him who strengthens me', but I need to receive that strengthening deep down in the wellsprings of my being if I am to be an enthusiastic servant. In the 'hour of Jesus' on Sunday, we receive his word from scripture and his body and blood through bread and wine. That hour is given to gather the Christian community to

God in Christ so that they can spring out refreshed into the service of a hungry and hurting world. There is a French military term, *'reculer pour mieux sauter'*, meaning 'coil up to better spring out'. In the same way, for the followers of Jesus our outgoing service is resourced by the regular gathering for worship.

Meditation

Strengthen for service, Lord, the hands
that holy things have taken;
let ears that now have heard thy songs
to clamour never waken.

Lord, may the tongues which 'Holy' sang
keep free from all deceiving;
the eyes which saw thy love be bright,
thy blessed hope perceiving.

The feet that tread thy holy courts
from light do thou not banish;
the bodies by thy Body fed
with thy new life replenish.

FOURTH-CENTURY SYRIAN HYMN[63]

Salt and light

Those who come close to Jesus are influenced by his selfless-ness. They receive, to give out in service. So how do they serve?

In the Sermon on the Mount, Jesus speaks of his followers seasoning and illuminating the world through good works that will point people to God:

'You are the salt of the earth; but if salt has lost its taste, how can its saltiness be restored? It is no longer good for anything, but is thrown out and trampled under foot. You are the light of the world. A city built on a hill cannot be hidden. No one after lighting a lamp puts it under the bushel basket, but on the lampstand, and it gives light to all in the house. In the same way, let your light shine before others, so that they may see your good works and give glory to your Father in heaven.' (Matthew 5:13–16)

When we read the Acts of the Apostles, we see the powerful impact of the first sharing of the good news of the death and resurrection of Jesus and the gift of the Holy Spirit on the day of Pentecost (Acts 2). As a result, those who believed joined together in communities that initially held all things in common. Eventually these communities were persecuted and, through that persecution, were split up to be scattered influentially right across the Roman empire. This presumably felt like a disaster at first, but it meant that the influence of those communities spread dramatically.

The story of St Pachomius gives us a glimpse of how Christian influence came to bear in the first centuries AD. Born in 292 in Egypt to pagan parents, Pachomius was forcibly recruited into the Roman army when he was 20. During a military campaign, the soldiers with whom he served were taken captive by enemy troops. One group of local people took pity on the captives and gave them meals. Puzzled at their generosity, Pachomius asked why they were doing it. 'They are Christians,' he was told. 'That is the sort of thing Christians do.' He was intrigued and wanted to know more. Baptised in 314, he became the founder of monastic communities in Egypt.

When we open our hands for service with Jesus, we work with fellow Christians in a way that should challenge the thinking of unbelievers and intrigue them so that they want to find out more. Christianity often appeals as a way of life before it appeals as a system of belief, although one flows from the other.

The origin of hospitals in the Western world traces back, in part, to followers of Jesus who cared for people who had infectious diseases, without regard to their own safety. This care was made possible by their faith that Jesus was mightier even than death, should that be their lot in consequence of serving where he led. Throughout the centuries after the decline of the Roman Empire, the torch of learning and civilisation was kept burning in monastic communities that were committed to a rule of study, with outcomes in the development of schools serving literacy and scientific knowledge across the Christian world. Besides the genesis of hospitals and schools, we can trace the rule of law in Western society to the Christian principle of the dignity of humankind made in the image of God. In these and other ways, followers of Jesus have seasoned and illuminated the world.

Meditation

I came to cast fire upon the earth
through lives I light up
and to season the world
through my disciples.
As catalysts stay unconsumed
yet speed chemical reactions,
so my Church remains eternally
while serving peace and justice
from generation to generation.
As Israel's calling served my plan for all nations,
so through a select few I bless the world today,
turning the wrath of humanity to my praise.

(SEE PSALM 76:10; ISAIAH 49:1–7; LUKE 12:49)

Making a difference

In the Gospels, we read how both men and women were drawn to Jesus because they had heard of the difference he was making to people's lives. He has not changed and can make all the difference in the world to people again and again and again.

Leatha worked in the local library. She was a lapsed Roman Catholic and her sister went to St Wilfrith's, the first church I served as a parish priest. Shortly after my arrival, we added an opportunity for healing ministry after Sunday evensong. Through her sister, Leatha came along to seek alleviation for a chronic chest condition. She came forward to the altar for the laying on of hands performed by myself with a group of church members. In the days that followed, she was remarkably healed. Out of gratitude she threw herself into the life of St Wilfrith's, where she served eventually as church treasurer. Her joining the followers of Jesus in the village caused a ripple effect and brought several friends into church or nearer to church. Like St Paul in his letter to the church in Rome, Leatha could say, 'I am not ashamed of the gospel; it is the power of God for salvation to everyone who has faith' (Romans 1:16).

Where there is life, there is growth. A church on the move is one where members are aware of the difference that Jesus is making in their individual lives and also in their local community. Opening our hands to Jesus can involve making them instruments of healing for others. In my present church, we were very isolated by the extreme cold weather early in 2010. Caroline served with her husband in the village 'dial a lift' scheme. Since they had a four-wheel-drive vehicle, they were able to help Lesley, who had cancer, obtain vital treatment at the local hospital. Caroline told me about Lesley's situation and I visited to offer her prayer, which was gratefully received. We celebrated the sacrament of anointing for her in church and I became aware of how Lesley's faith grew over the months. The acts of service of both Caroline and myself were in partnership with Jesus but in different ways. Her service was being helpful; mine was healing prayer. Both of us became channels for Jesus.

Both Leatha's joining the church and Lesley's growth in faith had an effect on other people close to them, as well as on the church and the community as people came to admit that prayer was really worthwhile. We return here to one of the central themes of this book: Jesus is a great connector. He always wants to use the gifts of his followers to connect people with God and build his body on earth. The dynamic that builds as a result fulfils the prophecy of Zechariah: 'Thus says the Lord of hosts: in those days ten men from nations of every language shall take hold of a Jew, grasping his garment and saying, "Let us go with you, for we have heard that God is with you"' (Zechariah 8:23).

There is reported to be a French village where there is a statue of Jesus that lost its hands in shelling during World War II. When peace returned, the villagers did not replace the hands of Jesus. Instead they put up a sign that read 'No hands but yours.'

Meditation

Christ has no body now on earth but yours,
no hands but yours,
no feet but yours;
yours are the eyes through which Christ's compassion
is to look out to the earth;
yours are the feet by which He is to go about doing good
and yours are the hands by which He is to bless us now.[64]

Jesus before you

We get to know more of Jesus by working alongside him, but it is also true that this work can be happening without our realising it. So much of our life flows along unselfconsciously. If we study Jesus, have an attitude of faith in him and worship him, his influence penetrates to the depths of our being so that our actions bear his fragrance. Sometimes we seem to carry the presence of Jesus with us. At other times we know that he is carrying us. On yet other occasions he is waiting ahead of us. He sees all we do—and also what we do not do.

In one of his last teachings before he died, Jesus spoke in a parable of the last judgment and his role in it:

When the Son of Man comes in his glory, and all the angels with him, then he will sit on the throne of his glory. All the nations will be gathered before him, and he will separate people one from another as a shepherd separates the sheep from the goats, and he will put the sheep at his right hand and the goats at the left. Then the king will say to those at his right hand, 'Come, you that are blessed by my Father, inherit the kingdom prepared for you from the foundation of the world; for I was hungry and you gave me food, I was thirsty and you gave me something to drink, I was a stranger and you welcomed me, I was naked and you gave me clothing, I was sick and you took care of me, I was in prison and you visited me.' Then the righteous will answer him, 'Lord, when was it that we saw you hungry and gave you food, or thirsty and gave you something to drink? And when was it that we saw you a stranger and welcomed you, or naked and gave you clothing? And when was it that we saw you sick or in prison and visited you?' And the king will answer them, 'Truly I tell you, just as you did it to one of the least of these who are members of my family, you did it to me.' (Matthew 25:31–40)

All the good works listed as done to 'the least' are said to have been done to the Lord. The parable continues as the king reproves those who neglected these works: in doing so, they were neglecting him.

I once talked with someone who had worked, for a time, close to Mother Teresa of Calcutta. As he went through the day, he was struck by Teresa's constantly attentive look. He saw this loving gaze when she looked down into her hands on receiving the bread of the Eucharist. The same gaze appeared when she took and held a newly arrived abandoned baby. Her attitude showed that she grasped something of the mystery that Jesus is before us both in the sacrament of Holy Communion and in the people we encounter. She taught those who worked with her to treat the next person they met as if he or she were Christ. In this way, the gathering at the Eucharist, 'the hour of Jesus', can be a school to help us gain eyes to see and worship Jesus hidden, whether in bread or in neighbour.

This is why C.S. Lewis writes, 'Next to the blessed sacrament itself, your neighbour is the holiest object presented to your senses'[65] and Jean Vanier writes:

There is an intimate connection between the presence of Jesus in the Eucharist and the presence of Jesus in the deprived person. The deprived person sends us back to Jesus in the Eucharist. To receive the body of Jesus is to have his eyes and his heart to see him in the poor.[66]

Meditation

Blessed and praised be Jesus Christ
upon his throne of glory,
in the most holy sacrament of the altar,
in the holy scriptures,
in the poor and needy
and in the hearts of all his faithful people,
now and always,
to the end of the ages. Amen

(SEE MATTHEW 25:40; 26:26; COLOSSIANS 1:25; 2 TIMOTHY 3:16; REVELATION 1:5)

In summary

When we meet Jesus, we find ourselves being drawn into partnership with the community of faith in serving God's kingdom. Through this service, Jesus expands our mind and heart towards his dimensions and aspirations, because service of others challenges our tendency to self-preoccupation. By pondering Jesus, we are influenced by one who 'emptied himself, taking the form of a slave' (Philippians 2:7).

Our enthusiasm for service links with our readiness both to give and to receive. It takes humility to put our hands in the hands of Jesus, but through that alliance we find that we can 'do all things through him who strengthens' us (Philippians 4:13). The followers of Jesus season and illuminate the world. Through imaginative service to others, they demonstrate an appealing way of life that draws others to seek the source of their love and energy. Jesus can make a visible transformation in the lives of those who are open to him. This healing and transformation has a ripple effect in the compassion for others that flows out of friendship with him.

Once the eye of faith is opened, we can see a link between the Jesus who is before us when we worship and the Jesus who is before us in the needy. We learn that he is waiting for us in daily life, especially in the people we meet.

For action

- Start the day by asking Jesus to guide you to those who most need your attention.
- Look back on your life and recognise the fruitfulness of occasions when you have let go of your own agenda to serve someone else.
- Find out from a church leader how you could receive spiritual direction or prayer healing ministry to be better guided in the use of your gifts, time and energy.
- Read through the judgment parable in Matthew 25:31–46 and prayerfully apply it to your life as a form of conscience examination.

CHAPTER 7

Open your life: The place of witness

Truth-telling and faith sit uncomfortably together. Believers can shrink back from witnessing because they lack either knowledge or the courage of their convictions. Non-believers may be poised to set the truth we tell against other claims and are often quick to expose hypocrisy.

When we meet with Jesus in the company of his followers, we grow in certain knowledge of his uniqueness. As that knowledge dawns upon us, so does its claim upon our lives; and as our lives open up to Jesus, we are made his witness.

- By reason we accept his existence and resurrection.
- By faith we see that he is Son of God and Saviour and welcome his Spirit.
- By worship and prayer we come into his presence to be drawn heavenwards.
- By fellowship with his people we are inspired and formed by the faith of the Church down the centuries.
- By service we forget our own agendas to work for his kingdom in the cause of justice, love and peace.

Our meeting with Jesus in all the ways we have examined in this book impels us to words and deeds that bear witness to him to all those we know. We learn to brave the discomfort of being a truth teller! As St Peter told the religious authorities in Jerusalem, 'For we cannot keep from speaking about what we have seen and heard' (Acts 4:20). St John later wrote:

We declare to you what was from the beginning, what we have heard, what we have seen with our eyes, what we have looked at and touched with our hands, concerning the word of life—this life was revealed, and we have seen it and testify to it, and declare to you the eternal life that was with the Father and was revealed to us—we declare to you what we have seen and heard so that you also may have fellowship with us; and truly our fellowship is with the Father and with his Son Jesus Christ. We are writing these things so that our joy may be complete. (1 John 1:1–4)

Both Peter and John were candid about the fact that their joy in Jesus would be incomplete until it was shared by everyone who could possibly be reached with it. For 20 centuries, that joy has rippled across the world and down through 80 generations. Today, at least two billion people identify with Christianity, which is a third of the total population of the planet.

If, by reason and faith, we are meeting with Jesus in worship, prayer, Christian fellowship and service, we cannot escape the responsibility that he will finally place on us to be his witnesses. This is made clear in the words of Jesus to the first disciples before he ascended to heaven:

Now the eleven disciples went to Galilee, to the mountain to which Jesus had directed them. When they saw him, they worshipped him; but some doubted. And Jesus came and said to them, 'All authority in heaven and on earth has been given to me. Go therefore and make disciples of all nations, baptising them in the name of the

Father and of the Son and of the Holy Spirit, and teaching them
to obey everything that I have commanded you. And remember, I
am with you always, to the end of the age.' (Matthew 28:16–20)

It is heartening to reflect that this commandment of Jesus
has been so fully obeyed—and also that the spread of the
gospel has come about, even if some have doubted in every
age.

To be a witness for Jesus involves gaining clarity about his
saving truth, and it involves listening to the people around
us so that we can speak helpfully of his salvation. We cannot
witness to Jesus effectively in our strength alone, which
is why he gives us spiritual gifts such as discernment and
healing. At the same time, we are called to be ready to put
our possessions and maybe even our lives on the line for the
sake of the gospel.

To be his witnesses, we need to open our lives to him as the
virgin Mary did, whose surrender to God's work led straight
on to her speaking out about it (Luke 1:26–38, 46–55).

The truth to be told

Jesus helps us face the truth both about ourselves and about
the world. As he does so, he opens up for us and for all a
vision of where we are ultimately going. Scripture tells us that
as God's Son, Jesus Christ made, redeemed and will have the
last say over the world. In the words of the Nicene Creed,
'He will come again in glory to judge the living and the dead.'

God made human beings for friendship with him, but
that friendship was lost as men and women put up a barrier
against him. Jesus came, as God made flesh, to break the

barrier of sin so that all who receive him can be restored to friendship. This is the good news of Jesus, but, like all good things, it comes at a price—that of facing up to our shortcomings and putting ourselves in our place before God: 'So you also must consider yourselves dead to sin and alive to God in Christ Jesus' (Romans 6:11).

Mortal beings cannot face death, let alone judgment. By coming among us, God has provided a way forward through these awesome realities for those who will accept his offer. This way forward is part of 'a plan for the fullness of time, to gather up all things in [Christ], things in heaven and things on earth' (Ephesians 1:10). Incidental to this plan is the fact that there is 'no condemnation for those who are in Christ Jesus' (Romans 8:1). Those who open their lives to Jesus are caught up in a forward movement that will take them right beyond this world and God's judgment upon it.

When we reflect on truths such as these, we might ask ourselves by what authority we lay hold of them. In the end, that authority has to be divine revelation, going beyond but not against reason. If Jesus is God made flesh, what he says and does has supreme authority. Unbelievably, that authority is given to his followers, so that, irrespective of our shortcomings, the Church can lift Jesus up before the world as Lord and Saviour, 'that repentance and forgiveness of sins... be proclaimed in his name to all nations' (Luke 24:47).

When we meet with Jesus, we become aware of very many who are missing out on the awesome truth that is in him. We yearn for them to own, with us, the divine purpose he reveals to those who give their lives to him. In the words of the 1966 Dutch Catechism:

The gospel often notes the deep sadness of those who cling to their old way of life and refuse to allow God entrance. It breaks out in 'murmurs' or groans of disapproval when Jesus eats with sinners (Luke 19:7), when he heals the sick (Mark 3:6) and when the children dance for joy in the Temple (Matthew 21:15). The workers who had been in the vineyard before the eleventh hour (Matthew 20:11) and the elder brother of the prodigal are also joyless. 'But it was fitting to make merry and be glad, for this your brother was dead, and is alive; he was lost, and is found' (Luke 15:32). The joy is the joy of those who do not feel sure of their own excellence, but of God's grace... Jesus makes no pronouncement on the number of the saved. But he does say that there are very many who refuse to respond or who spoil the gift of themselves by their half-heartedness, and that they thereby refuse joy, perhaps their eternal joy.[67]

Just as good parents respect and cultivate a growth of freedom and independence in their child, so it seems to be with God as heavenly Father. No one is forced to do as he says, but he delights in the good choices of his children, especially as they respond to the great love he has shown the world in the sacrifice of Jesus his Son.

Meditation

My God, I love Thee; not because
I hope for heaven thereby,
nor yet because who love Thee not
are lost eternally.

Thou, O my Jesus, Thou didst me
upon the cross embrace;
for me didst bear the nails and spear,
and manifold disgrace.

Then why, O blessed Jesus Christ,
should I not love Thee well?
Not for the hope of winning heaven,
nor of escaping hell.

Not with the hope of gaining aught,
nor seeking a reward,
but as Thyself hast loved me,
O everlasting Lord! [68]

....

Listening love

The Irish priest and writer John O'Donohue wrote much that engages with the spiritual seekers of our day. In an article for a spirituality journal, he says:

Our age has an obsession with images and appearances to the forsaking of presence and reality. People are running away from themselves at the deeper level as they are carried away in the flow of trivia… the power of the media is such as to have drawn us out into a fantasy world which draws out our energies of attention only to dull them and control them… In the end the most effective and trustable witness is the integrity of individual presence. [69]

Jesus is real presence—more real than any being, the very ground and foundation of being. The good news of Jesus has rightly been expressed in myriad words and images through the ages but, as O'Donohue wisely comments, 'the most effective and trustable witness is the integrity of individual presence'.

Janet was one of my churchwardens in St Wilfrith's. She was a great listener, someone to whom people came to share their problems and heartaches. In a period of change for the church, she became a powerful force for building up love and understanding in the congregation. Looking back, I can see that it was the love poured into the church through people like Janet that, coupled with the recovery of faith in God's healing power, served to bring about remarkable growth in numbers. Even her early death from cancer was turned to good—terrible loss though it was—as the outshining of her faith in the face of death inspired others to offer themselves for service. Her joyous Requiem Eucharist sowed many seeds of faith.

The world needs listeners in some ways more than it needs overt evangelists. Some of the most effective evangelism occurs when people receive attention from a follower of Jesus who may not at the time be pointing directly to the Lord. There is famous advice attributed to St Francis of Assisi to spread the good news of Jesus: 'Preach the gospel always. If necessary, use words!'

As we have already seen, we live in a culture that is very suspicious of any kind of religious faith. This is why the advice of St James is so important for shaping Christian witness: 'If any think they are religious, and do not bridle their tongues but deceive their hearts, their religion is worthless. Religion that is pure and undefiled before God, the Father, is this: to care for orphans and widows in their distress, and to keep oneself unstained by the world' (James 1:26–27). Witnessing to Jesus in both deed and word serves to infuse the world with the grace and love of God. By contrast, 'I will tell you' forms of witness can sound unconvincing and can, sadly, serve to put people off the good news altogether.

A story tells of a clergyman congratulating the comedian Groucho Marx: 'Thank you, Mr Marx, for all the enjoyment you have brought into the world.' The comedian replied, 'And thanks, Father, for all the enjoyment you've taken out of it!' Our calling is to witness to the truth that Christianity is convivial and life-giving, as Jesus himself makes clear: 'I have come that they may have life, and have it to the full' (John 10:10, NIV).

Meditation

A young boy was trying to open up a flower
whose buds were closed.
No matter how careful he tried to be,
he could not avoid damaging the bud as he forced it open.
'Why can't I open the flower like God does?' he asked.
'God opens the flower from the inside
and he only does this when there is warmth and light.'

Gifts of the Spirit

In Ephesians 3:14–20, St Paul speaks of the indwelling Jesus grounding believers with the whole Church—'with all the saints'—in the fullness of his love with its 'breadth and length and height and depth'. He goes on to speak of God's associated 'power at work within us... able to accomplish abundantly far more than all we can ask or imagine'. This power links to the Spirit-given authority that the followers of Jesus bear as his witnesses. As Paul writes elsewhere, 'We are ambassadors for Christ' (2 Corinthians 5:20), having received a commission from the power for whom we act (see Matthew 28:16–20).

The 19th-century Bishop of Durham, Joseph Lightfoot, said in an ordination address:

The ambassador, before acting, receives a commission from the power for whom he acts. The ambassador, while acting, acts not only as an agent, but as a representative of his sovereign. Lastly, the ambassador's duty is not merely to deliver a definite message, to carry out a definite policy; but he is obliged to watch opportunities, to study characters, to cast about for expedients, so that he may place it before his hearers in its most attractive form. He is a diplomatist.[70]

In other words, the empowering we have as Christians gives us confidence to speak the truth but in humility, with prudent loving consideration. The authority and the power of the Holy Spirit complement his gifts to us of humility and discernment. This empowerment for his followers was made clear by Jesus before he ascended to his Father: 'You will receive power when the Holy Spirit has come upon you; and you will be my witnesses' (Acts 1:8). The writer of the letter to the Hebrews further underlines the way the gifts of the Holy Spirit facilitate Christian witness: '[The message] was declared at first through the Lord, and it was attested to us by those who heard him, while God added his testimony by signs and wonders and various miracles, and by gifts of the Holy Spirit, distributed according to his will' (Hebrews 2:3–4).

Faith in Action is a Sussex-based charity that collects good-quality clothes, boxes them and pays for the boxes to be sent to Africa. My own church of St Giles, Horsted Keynes, is very much involved in collecting, packing and raising funds for transporting the clothes. One of those privileged to distribute the clothes in Africa spoke in St Giles of a church service where, unexpectedly, several thousand people turned up for a distribution of the boxes. She could see from the size of the crowd and the number of boxes that many would be disappointed. Distribution went ahead but, astonishingly, no one was disappointed. Somehow there were enough boxes so that 'God added his testimony by signs and wonders' to the generous action of our church.

I can think of a number of occasions when I have talked with people and been led to offer prayer for healing as a consequence. Most times the offer is accepted and, on occasion, this has led to an evident healing and to an increase of trust in Jesus in the person concerned. To me, this is a clear example of a gift of the Spirit bearing fruit in an individual life, deepening my faith and willingness to follow God's prompting, while bringing greater wholeness to the one prayed for. My faith in Jesus has also deepened through the times when I have gone to confession or spiritual direction and the priest or director has received God-given insight into my situation, in a way that has been challenging yet affirming.

Where we expect the Holy Spirit to work, he is ready to honour that expectancy and associated faith. The power of Jesus within us operates by the Holy Spirit to make us 'able to accomplish abundantly far more than all we can ask or imagine' (Ephesians 3:20). This power links to intercessory prayer, as Ole Hallesby writes: 'It is by prayer that we couple the powers of heaven to our helplessness... the powers which can awaken those who sleep in sin and raise the dead, the power which can capture strongholds and make the impossible possible.' [71]

Speaking the truth in love is something for which Jesus equips us as we open our lives to his Holy Spirit in persistent prayer.

Meditation

'I say to you,
Ask, and it will be given to you;
search, and you will find;
knock, and the door will be opened for you.
For everyone who asks receives, and everyone who searches finds,
and for everyone who knocks, the door will be opened.
Is there anyone among you who, if your child asks for a fish,
will give a snake instead of a fish?
Or if the child asks for an egg, will give a scorpion?
If you then, who are evil,
know how to give good gifts to your children,
how much more will the heavenly Father
give the Holy Spirit to those who ask him!'

LUKE 11:9–13

Mary: a model for us to follow

When we meet Jesus, we eventually meet up with his mother Mary and all the saints whose presence with us is the fruit of his resurrection. Mary is the very first witness to Jesus, the one who first presented him to the world. She teaches Christians in any age five qualities essential to handing on the truth that is in Jesus.

To be contemplative

When the angel Gabriel came to Mary to announce her divine motherhood, she 'pondered what sort of greeting this might be', and the account of Christ's birth ends with the comment, 'His mother treasured all these things in her heart' (Luke 1:29; 2:51). During her pregnancy, Mary visited her cousin Elizabeth, also pregnant, whose unborn child leapt in her womb as a response to encountering Jesus in Mary's womb (Luke 1:39–45). It was as if the depths within Mary—Jesus—shone forth invisibly to Elizabeth and her child, John the Baptist.

Mary provides here an image of Christian contemplation. As we contemplate Christ, his presence grows within us. If God is in us—and God is, of course, bigger than we are—his presence eventually grows to reveal itself outside of us. To be a witness to Jesus involves words and deeds, but these can only flow from within the kind of open heart that Mary demonstrates and keeps before the followers of Jesus.

To be visionary

When her cousin Elizabeth greeted her, Mary's response was a song that has found a daily place in the worship of the Christian Church:

My soul magnifies the Lord,
and my spirit rejoices in God my Saviour,
for he has looked with favour on the lowliness of his servant.
Surely, from now on all generations will call me blessed;
for the Mighty One has done great things for me,
and holy is his name.
His mercy is for those who fear him
from generation to generation.
He has shown strength with his arm;
he has scattered the proud in the thoughts of their hearts.
He has brought down the powerful from their thrones,
and lifted up the lowly;
he has filled the hungry with good things,
and sent the rich away empty.
He has helped his servant Israel,
in remembrance of his mercy,
according to the promise he made to our ancestors,
to Abraham and to his descendants for ever.'

LUKE 1:46–55

This song, named Magnificat, after its opening words when sung in Latin, is full of great expectations. It is an invitation towards a cosmic vision of God rather than one restricted to human dimensions, picking up on the angel Gabriel's promise that 'nothing will be impossible with God'. (Luke 1:37) 'The Mighty One has done great things for us, and holy is his name': where there is faithful witness to Jesus and his good news, great things surely follow.

To be visionary is to have confidence to welcome the great things that are the gift of a great God. Recognising our own littleness in the face of God's greatness is a balancing school of humility, which corrects the tendency to size God down to our 'manageable' proportions. Life with Jesus, as Mary shows us, is a lifelong eye-opener to the vision of the all-powerful and ever-loving God whose joyful goodness endures for all eternity.

To be obedient

'Mary said [to the angel Gabriel], "Here am I, the servant of the Lord; let it be with me according to your word"' (Luke 1:38). Through her act of obedience and self-surrender, Jesus came into the world by the Holy Spirit. Jesus himself waited 30 years before his public ministry began, and Mary waited obediently alongside him. Effective witness to the saving power of Jesus today can require similar patience, as we wait, obedient to circumstances, for the right sorts of occasions to speak of God to other people.

St John records the start of Jesus' ministry, when Mary was present with him at a marriage in Cana where the wine ran out. Her attentiveness to their host's embarrassment demonstrated obedience to serving the demands of these circumstances. She also deferred with expectation to her son, calling on the servants to obey him, saying, 'Do whatever he tells you' (John 2:5). In consequence, 30 gallons of water were turned into wine. Through her obedience, Mary kept walking within God's will and brought consequent blessings to others.

Speaking of the mission of the Christian Church in our own day, Archbishop Rowan Williams has this to say: 'Mission is finding out what God is doing and joining in.'[72] Mary reminds us of the importance of keeping close to Jesus and being ready to surrender our own ambitions to his. Through her example, we can be reminded of how much we need to be similarly self-surrendering.

To be of the Holy Spirit

Mary conceived Christ by the Holy Spirit, and her joy in the same Spirit expresses itself in her Magnificat. Years later, she gathered with the infant church to pray for the Spirit as Jesus had commanded: 'All these were constantly devoting themselves to prayer, together with certain women, including Mary the mother of Jesus' (Acts 1:14).

If Jesus came into the world 'from the Holy Spirit and the Virgin Mary' (to use the words of the Nicene Creed), so today he brings new followers to birth as the Christian community opens itself, as Mary did, to the Spirit's power. We have reflected already upon the baptism in the Spirit and the importance of building expectant faith in Jesus, trusting that the Spirit will empower us for witness, just as he promised the first believers (Acts 1:8).

Mary's life underlines how much witness to Jesus relies on the Holy Spirit. In the words of St Paul, 'our message of the gospel came to you not in word only, but also in power and in the Holy Spirit and with full conviction' (1 Thessalonians 1:5).

To be of the Church

Mary was present for the nine days of prayer before the Holy Spirit came at Pentecost, as, after the ascension of Jesus, his disciples constantly devoted themselves to prayer. It is logical to believe that she was there at Pentecost to experience the answer to that prayer. For her, it would be a second anointing when the church was brought to birth by the descent of the Holy Spirit that morning.

In receiving the Spirit afresh with the other disciples at Pentecost, the mother of Jesus reminds us that the Holy Spirit is given not primarily to individuals but to the Church as a whole. The disciples' solidarity in prayer, in receiving the Spirit and then in witness mirrors the first reception of Jesus by his mother, which overflowed in the gospel witness of her Magnificat. Jesus, who came first to live in Mary, comes to live in all his disciples now that his risen power is made available to them by the descent of the Spirit.

Reflection on Mary reminds us how Jesus first came to dwell in a human life and is a pointer to his will to be alongside those who welcome him in every age, as well as his desire to set them alight within his Spirit-anointed community. Inspired and challenged by Mary's example, the Church of Jesus Christ can work to be lighthouses in the darkness of the world, to generate communities that draw people to the contemplation of Jesus and the transformation that follows.

Meditation

Jesus, living in Mary, live in me!
Turn my gaze with hers to you.
Let her submission be mine:
'Behold I am your servant.
Let it be done to me as you will!'
As you overshadowed Mary with your Spirit,
overshadow me and join me
in your praise and service
to your whole church,
so the world may be set alight
and your kingdom come.

(SEE LUKE 1:28, 38, 42)

In summary

If we meet with Jesus in prayer and worship, scripture, Christian fellowship and service, we will become his witnesses. This is what he wants of all his followers, as he makes clear in these commissioning words to his disciples: 'Go therefore and make disciples of all nations, baptising them in the name of the Father and of the Son and of the Holy Spirit, and teaching them to obey everything that I have commanded you' (Matthew 28:19–20). Believers witness to Jesus because he tells them to do so, because he wants his Church to grow and because experiencing his love produces a joy that naturally overflows to transform all that he touches.

Telling the truth about Jesus is inseparable from a loving commitment to dialogue. If Christian witnesses do not listen to other people, they fall short of the example of Jesus himself. We are ambassadors for Jesus, authorised to speak for him but with a humility that is diplomatic and presents his case in the most compelling form. Through prayer, the Holy Spirit adds his supernatural gifts to ours in presenting both the challenge and the invitation of Jesus.

As we continue on our way as disciples of Jesus today, we can draw inspiration from the virgin Mary's qualities of contemplation, vision, obedience, openness to the Spirit and communion with the Church, summarising the ideal for effective Christian witness.

For action

- Write your own summary of the good news of Jesus in no more than 100 words.
- Identify something that Jesus has done for you that you can share naturally and confidently with others at an appropriate moment.
- Reflect on your life from time to time to identify missed opportunities to witness, and reflect upon times when your witness seems to have been ineffective.
- Take courage on occasion to offer to pray with people who share their needs with you.

❖

Afterword

Is life a terminal disease or an investment? What lies beyond the last chapter? Is the book of life really a prologue? If so, where is the evidence and who has authoritative guidance?

Meet Jesus: no one else is better equipped to speak of the world to come! It is literally reasonable to hold to the truth not only of his existence but also of his resurrection. Both invite us to put faith in him as the unique revelation of God, our maker, saviour and would-be friend. In this book I have described how friendship with Jesus grows through worship, prayer, fellowship, service and witness. Friends light up one another's lives, but the inspiration that Jesus gives to his friends is literally out of this world. Over the course of my life, I have been opening my heart to Jesus in fits and starts and discovering in him a loyalty and a power that take me out of myself into 'the life that really is life' (1 Timothy 6:19). To see that life growing within and around us is the special gift of Jesus to all who turn from self and sin to him as Son of God, saviour and baptiser in the Holy Spirit.

Meeting Jesus brings us into the community of the resurrection through 'the apostles' teaching and fellowship, the breaking of bread and the prayers' (Acts 2:42). It is a common life that anticipates here on earth the joys of the world to come. If we give ourselves in friendship to Jesus, his heart becomes ours—the heart for God and for the world, with the aspiration that 'the kingdom of the world... become the kingdom of our Lord and of his Christ' (Revelation 11:15, NIV).

This is a cause that will outlast every one of us and the universe itself!

Now may the God of peace, who brought back from the dead our Lord Jesus, the great shepherd of the sheep, by the blood of the eternal covenant, make you complete in everything good so that you may do his will, working among us that which is pleasing in his sight, through Jesus Christ, to whom be the glory for ever and ever. Amen. (Hebrews 13:20–21)

❖

Appendix

The Apostles' Creed

I believe in God, the Father almighty,
creator of heaven and earth.

I believe in Jesus Christ, his only Son, our Lord,
who was conceived by the Holy Spirit,
born of the Virgin Mary,
suffered under Pontius Pilate,
was crucified, died, and was buried;
he descended to the dead.
On the third day he rose again;
he ascended into heaven,
he is seated at the right hand of the Father,
and he will come to judge the living and the dead.

I believe in the Holy Spirit,
the holy catholic Church,
the communion of saints,
the forgiveness of sins,
the resurrection of the body,
and the life everlasting.
Amen.

COMMON WORSHIP

The Nicene Creed

We believe in one God,
the Father, the Almighty,
maker of heaven and earth,
of all that is,
seen and unseen.

We believe in one Lord, Jesus Christ,
the only Son of God,
eternally begotten of the Father,
God from God, Light from Light,
true God from true God,
begotten, not made,
of one Being with the Father;
through him all things were made.
For us and for our salvation he came down from heaven,
was incarnate from the Holy Spirit and the Virgin Mary
and was made man.
For our sake he was crucified under Pontius Pilate;
he suffered death and was buried.
On the third day he rose again
in accordance with the Scriptures;
he ascended into heaven
and is seated at the right hand of the Father.
He will come again in glory to judge the living and the dead,
and his kingdom will have no end.

We believe in the Holy Spirit,
the Lord, the giver of life,
who proceeds from the Father and the Son,

who with the Father and the Son is worshipped and glorified,
who has spoken through the prophets.
We believe in one holy catholic and apostolic Church.
We acknowledge one baptism for the forgiveness of sins.
We look for the resurrection of the dead,
and the life of the world to come.
Amen.

COMMON WORSHIP

The Sacraments

- Baptism
- Eucharist
- Anointing
- Confession
- Confirmation
- Marriage
- Ordination

The Ten Commandments

1 I am the Lord your God: you shall have no other gods but me.
2 You shall not make for yourself any idol, whether in the form of anything that is in heaven above, or that is on the earth beneath, or that is in the water under the earth. You shall not bow down to them or worship them.
3 You shall not take the name of the Lord your God in vain.

4 Remember the Sabbath day, and keep it holy. For six days you shall labour and do all your work. But the seventh day is a Sabbath to the Lord your God.

5 Honour your father and your mother.

6 You shall not murder.

7 You shall not commit adultery.

8 You shall not steal.

9 You shall not bear false witness.

10 You shall not covet.

COMMON WORSHIP

The Lord's Prayer

Our Father, who art in heaven,
hallowed be thy name;
thy kingdom come;
thy will be done;
on earth as it is in heaven.
Give us this day our daily bread.
And forgive us our trespasses,
as we forgive those who trespass against us.
And lead us not into temptation,
but deliver us from evil.
For thine is the kingdom,
the power and the glory,
for ever and ever.
Amen.

COMMON WORSHIP

❖

How to use this book with groups

Meet Jesus group session 1: The place of reason

- Opening prayer
- Read Acts 17:16–34, which shows Paul's eagerness to engage in reasoned debate about Jesus with the Athenians.
- Silence
- Read session aims:

    + To help participants establish for themselves the reasonable basis of Christianity.
    + To address one or two of the questions raised in the chapter which touch on major obstacles to Christian belief.
    + To begin to identify ways forward that would help people to engage intellectually with what Jesus is all about.

- General feedback from reading *Meet Jesus* Chapter 1 in twos or threes
- Plenary feedback
- Group discussion of three or four of these questions or topics:

    + Do you believe there is a reasonable basis for Christianity?
    + Does Christianity put people in their right mind?
    + Consider the evidence from outside the Bible for Jesus' existence. Is it convincing?

- ✦ Does the New Testament have a ring of historical truth about it?
- ✦ If you cannot prove God, where is the evidence for his existence?
- ✦ Is our instinct for right and wrong evidence for God's image within us?
- ✦ Share what you consider the best evidence for the resurrection of Jesus.
- ✦ What do you make of the discrepancies in the resurrection narratives?
- ✦ Does saying 'yes' to Jesus mean saying 'no' to other faiths?
- ✦ In what areas might other faiths wake Christians up to their own faith?

- Identify ways forward that would help people to engage intellectually with what Jesus is all about.
- Read one of the Chapter 1 meditations.
- Silence and concluding prayer.

Meet Jesus group session 2: The place of faith

- Opening prayer.
- Read John 1:1–18, which speaks of how Jesus is revealed to faith as God's Son who has come into the world.
- Silence
- Read session aims:

  + To help participants understand Christian faith as the acceptance in Jesus of the definitive revelation of God.
  + To gain clarity about the saving work of Jesus witnessed to in the Bible, the call to repent, believe and be baptised, and the associated understanding of God as a Trinity.
  + To begin to identify ways forward that would help people build faith in Jesus as Lord and Saviour.

- General feedback from reading *Meet Jesus* Chapter 2 in twos or threes
- Plenary feedback
- Group discussion of three or four of these questions or topics:

  + Do you see faith and reason as complementary or competing?
  + Share any experiences of the awakening of faith in Jesus as God's Son.
  + What do you see as good about the good news of Jesus?
  + What is the best explanation for the suffering and death of Jesus?
  + How do you see the role of the Holy Spirit in relation to Jesus?
  + 'You may possess the Spirit—but does he possess you?' Discuss.

+ In what sense is belief in the Trinity logical?
+ Do you agree that belief in the Trinity witnesses to God as personal?
+ How does holy scripture serve day-by-day repentance towards God?
+ In what sense is the Bible true?

- Identify ways forward that would help people build faith in Jesus as Lord and Saviour.
- Read one of the Chapter 2 meditations.
- Silence and concluding prayer.

Meet Jesus group session 3: The place of worship

- Opening prayer
- Read Revelation 5:6–14, which gives a picture of heavenly worship surrounding Jesus the sacrificial Lamb.
- Silence
- Read session aims:

  + To help participants see how meeting Jesus in worship draws people into God's praise and service.
  + To gain appreciation of the sacraments as worshipful encounters with Jesus, especially the Eucharist and the ministry of reconciliation, as well as the value of the gifts of the Holy Spirit in worship.
  + To begin to identify ways forward that would help improve worship locally and people's attention to God within it.

- General feedback from reading *Meet Jesus* Chapter 3 in twos or threes
- Plenary feedback
- Group discussion of three or four of these questions or topics:

  + Share experiences of uplifting worship.
  + How demanding is worship in your experience?
  + Do you see Jesus behind the action of the sacraments? If not, why not?
  + How important is the involvement of our bodies in worship?
  + In what way does the Eucharist show forth the death of Jesus?

+ Do you agree with the view that the Eucharist has a cosmic dimension?
+ Why is the confession of sin so important within worship?
+ Share any experiences of receiving the assurance of God's forgiveness.
+ How does repetition of set prayers help us meet Jesus in worship?
+ Share experiences of Jesus in worship through the gifts of the Spirit.

• Identify ways forward that would help improve worship locally and people's attention to God within it.
• Read one of the Chapter 3 meditations.
• Silence and concluding prayer.

Meet Jesus group session 4: The place of prayer

- Opening prayer
- Read Ephesians 3:14–21, which describes prayer as a heart-to-heart relationship with Jesus Christ.
- Silence
- Read session aims:

  + To help participants become more drawn to meeting Jesus in prayer.
  + To gain insight into Christian prayer as a relationship as well as a discipline, with attention to praying from scripture, contemplation, self-examination and the Jesus Prayer.
  + To begin to identify ways forward that would help improve personal prayer.

- General feedback from reading *Meet Jesus* Chapter 4 in twos or threes
- Plenary feedback
- Group discussion of three or four of these questions or topics:

  + How would you define prayer?
  + Share any experience of God that prayer has brought you.
  + Do you find that your prayer involves listening to God?
  + What sort of answers do you obtain from your prayer?
  + In what ways do you find the Bible an inspiration for prayer?
  + Do you find a physical focus for prayer useful?
  + Is it easy for you to find God in silence?

- ✦ Do you find that your prayer has helped your self-knowledge?
- ✦ Share helpful ways of overcoming mental distractions in prayer.
- ✦ How valuable do you see repetition in prayer, as in the Jesus Prayer?

- Identify ways forward that might help improve personal prayer.
- Read one of the Chapter 4 meditations.
- Silence and concluding prayer.

Meet Jesus group session 5: The place of fellowship

- Opening prayer
- Read Acts 2:37–47, which tells how fellowship within the Church follows from commitment to Jesus.
- Silence
- Read session aims:

  + To help participants see how fellowship with Jesus is inseparable from commitment to the whole Christian fellowship.
  + To gain understanding of how the fellowship of the Church serves communion with Jesus and the authoritative and inspirational communication of his teaching, despite the Church's failings and the world's indifference to truth.
  + To begin to identify ways forward that would help develop the quality of church life locally so that it displays more of the life of Jesus.

- General feedback from reading *Meet Jesus* Chapter 5 in twos or threes
- Plenary feedback
- Group discussion of three or four of these questions or topics:

  + Can you be a Christian without church membership?
  + What gifts come to us from Jesus through his Church?
  + How do you balance the authority of scripture, tradition and reason?
  + Where do you see good use of authority in the Church?
  + Where do you see misuse of authority in the Church?

+ Is it possible to be sure of Jesus without appearing arrogant?
+ How upset should a follower of Jesus be at their shortcomings?
+ Is it true that lack of Christian fellowship makes Jesus feel less real?
+ What causes the teachings of the local and universal church to clash?
+ Are there things that people would find intriguing in your church?

- Identify ways forward that would help develop the quality of church life locally so that it displays more of the life of Jesus.
- Read one of the Chapter 5 meditations.
- Silence and concluding prayer.

Meet Jesus group session 6: The place of service

- Opening prayer
- Read Matthew 25:31–40, which speaks of meeting Jesus in the service of the needy.
- Silence
- Read session aims:

  + To help participants see how Jesus is encountered in the service of other people.
  + To gain understanding of how Jesus draws us into the service of God's kingdom, challenging our self-preoccupation and coming alongside us to help us make a difference to the world around us.
  + To begin to identify ways forward that would build up the servant ministries of individuals and the local church.

- General feedback from reading *Meet Jesus* Chapter 6 in twos or threes
- Plenary feedback
- Group discussion of three or four of these questions or topics:

  + How much do you see Jesus as a practical saviour and helper?
  + Share occasions when God's Spirit has prompted you to serve others.
  + Does forgetting yourself, to serve others, make Jesus more real to you?
  + What are the things that hold people back from serving others?

- + In what ways do Christians locally act as 'salt and light'?
- + What do you think Jesus would do to serve needy people near you?
- + Share occasions when you have seen Christian service helping people find Jesus.
- + Can you recall a time when helping someone to voice a prayer has been a service?
- + Do you see a link between Jesus in the Eucharist and Jesus in the needy?
- + In what ways can we find spiritual direction to improve our ministry of service?

- Identify ways forward that would build up the servant ministries of individuals and the local church.
- Read one of the Chapter 6 meditations.
- Silence and concluding prayer.

Meet Jesus group session 7: The place of witness

- Opening prayer
- Read Acts 1:6–11, in which Jesus tells his followers that they will be his witnesses.
- Silence
- Read session aims:

  + To help participants see that meeting Jesus empowers them to be his witnesses.
  + To gain understanding of how Christian faith is truth to be told in a convivial way, as the Holy Spirit leads, and how the virgin Mary is a model witness for us to follow.
  + To begin to identify ways forward that would build courage to witness to Jesus.

- General feedback from reading *Meet Jesus* Chapter 7 in twos or threes
- Plenary feedback
- Group discussion of three or four of these questions or topics:

  + Share occasions when your witness to Jesus appeared to succeed.
  + Share occasions when your witness to Jesus appeared to fail.
  + How much do you feel non-Christians are missing out?
  + Why should listening come before speaking in evangelism?
  + Share times when saying a prayer with someone has had a good effect.
  + Have you seen intercession open a door for you to share about Jesus?

- ✦ Are there occasions when you have braved fears to speak of Jesus?
- ✦ 'Mission is finding out what God is doing and joining in.' Discuss.
- ✦ What is most attractive about the witness to Jesus of the virgin Mary?
- ✦ Prepare and then speak for two minutes about what Jesus means to you.

- Identify ways forward that would build courage to witness to Jesus.
- Read one of the Chapter 7 meditations.
- Silence and concluding prayer.

Notes

1. Teilhard de Chardin, *Le Milieu Divin* (Fontana, 1967), p. 127.

2. C.S. Lewis, *Miracles* (Fount, 1977 edn), pp. 134–135.

3. George Wells, *Did Jesus Really Exist?* (Prometheus, 1975).

4. Tacitus, *Annals* 13.32, in Henry Bettenson (ed.), *Documents of the Christian Church* (OUP, 1963), p. 1.

5. Suetonius, *Vita Claudii* 25.4 in Bettenson, *Documents of the Christian Church*, p. 2.

6. Flavius Josephus, *Antiquities* 18.63, Arabic summary from Agapios' Kitab al-'Unwan at:
   http://ccat.sas.upenn.edu/~humm/Topics/JewishJesus/josephus.html.

7. Pliny the Younger, *Epistle to Trajan* 96, in Bettenson, *Documents of the Christian Church*, pp. 3–4.

8. *Works of Lucian, Volume 4, The Death of Peregrine* at www.sacred-texts.com/cla/luc/wl4/wl420.htm.

9. N.T. Wright, *Jesus and the Victory of God* (SPCK, 1996), p. xvi.

10. John Twisleton & James Dingemans, *A Case for God and Christianity* (2007), pamphlet available at www.premier.org.uk/features/archive/acaseforgodandchristianity.aspx

11. Timothy Keller, *The Reason for God* (Hodder & Stoughton, 2008), p. 25.

12. Karl Rahner, *The Eternal Year* (Helicon, 1964).

13. Simon Greenleaf, *The Testimony of the Evangelists* (Baker, 1984) p. vii, quoted in Lee Strobel, *The Case for Christ* (Zondervan, 1998), pp. 45–46.

14. 1988 Lambeth Conference report, quoted in Alec Graham (ed.), *The Mystery of Salvation* (CHP, 1997), p. 145.

15. Austin Flannery, *Vatican II Documents: Declaration on Non-Christians* (Geoffrey Chapman, 1972), p. 662.

16. Christopher Partridge (ed.), *The World's Religions* (Lion, 2010).

17. John Paul II, *Faith and Reason* (Catholic Truth Society, 1998), p. 3.

18. St Augustine, *Confessions* (Henry Chadwick, trans.), (OUP, 2008).

19. St Thomas Aquinas, *The Summa Theologica* (Benziger, 1947).

20. Thomas Merton, *Seeds of Contemplation* (Dell, 1958), p. 84.

21. Lord Chief Justice Darling, quoted by Michael Green, *Man Alive!* (IVP, 1969), p. 54.

22. John Polkinghorne, *Quantum Physics & Theology* (SPCK, 2007).

23. Ian Petit OSB, *You Will Receive Power* (DLT, 1994), p. 117.

24. Metropolitan Ignatios of Latakia, main theme address in The Uppsala Report 1968, quoted by Thomas J. Norris, *The Trinity: Life of God, Hope for Humanity: Towards a Theology of Communion* (New City Press, 2009), p. 41.

25. John Thomas Clark (ed.), *Stepping Stones: The Complete Bible Narratives* (Grosset & Dunlap, 1954).

26. Robert Backhouse (comp.), *5000 Quotations for Teachers & Preachers* (Kingsway, 1994), pp. 15–16.

27. Backhouse, *5000 Quotations*, p. 18.

28. Anglican-Roman Catholic International Commission, The Final Report (CTS/SPCK, 1982), p. 14.

29. 'O saving Victim, opening wide' (trans. J.M. Neale, 1818–66), Hymn 269 Part 2, *New English Hymnal* (Canterbury Press, 1990).

30. The Westminster Shorter Catechism of 1647, in Philip Schaff, *The Creeds of Christendom, Vol. 3: Creeds of the Evangelical Protestant Churches* (Harper & Brothers, 1878).

31. Evelyn Underhill, *Worship* (Nisbet, 1937), p. 5.

32. Catechism in The Book of Common Prayer (OUP, 1993), p. 356.

33. Pope Benedict XVI, Homily at Mass on World Youth Day, Cologne, 21 August 2005.

34. *The Sunday Missal* (Collins, 1975), p. 185.

35. Alexander Schmemann, *The World as Sacrament* (DLT, 1965).

36. Festo Kivengere, *I Love Idi Amin* (Marshall, Morgan and Scott, 1977).

37. Henri de Lubac SJ, *The Religion of Teilhard de Chardin* (Collins, 1967), p. 124.

38. Anthony de Mello, *Sadhana* (Image, 1984), pp. 119–120.

39. Br David Steindl Rast, in *Monastic Studies* (Mount Saviour Monastery, 1969); also recorded at www.gratefulness.org.

40. St Ignatius of Loyola, Spiritual Exercises, Prayer of offering from 'Contemplation for obtaining love', quoted in Robert Faricy & Lucy Rooney, *Knowing Jesus in the World* (St Pauls, 1999), p. 123.

41. See Joseph Tetlow (trans.), *The Spiritual Exercises of Ignatius Loyola* (Crossroad, 2009)

42. Walter Hooper (ed.), *Daily Readings with C.S. Lewis* (Fount, 1992), p. 66.

43. Raniero Cantalamessa, *The Power of the Cross* (DLT, 1996).

44. Jean-Pierre de Caussade, *Self-Abandonment to Divine Providence* (Fontana, 1976), p. 65.

45. Sergius Bulgakov, quoted by Timothy Ware, *The Orthodox Church* (Penguin, 1967), p. 313.

46. E. Kadloubovsky & G.E.H. Palmer (trans.), *Writings from the Philokalia on Prayer of the Heart* (Faber & Faber, 1977), p. 228.

47. Kadloubovsky & Palmer, *Writings from the Philokalia*, pp. 75–76.

48. Kadloubovsky & Palmer, *Writings from the Philokalia*, p. 228.

49. R.M. French (trans.), *The Way of a Pilgrim* (SPCK, 1965), p. 5.

50. Bishop Kallistos of Diokleia, *The Power of the Name* (SLG Press, 2007), p. 8.

51. A Monk of the Eastern Church, *On the Invocation of the Name of Jesus* (Fellowship of St Alban and St Sergius, 1949), p. 26.

52. French, *Way of a Pilgrim*, p. 31.

53. Kadloubovsky & Palmer, *Writings from the Philokalia*, p. 319.

54. C.S. Lewis, *The Screwtape Letters* (Collins, 1979 edition), pp. 14–15.

55. Articles of Religion in The Book of Common Prayer.

56. World Council of Churches, *Baptism, Eucharist and Ministry* (1982), p. 14.

57. The Church of England Declaration of Assent, required of church officers.

58. In-flight press interview with Pope Benedict XVI en route to Portugal in the context of the paedophile priests scandal widely reported in the media, 11 May 2010.

59. This popular quote from Bridget Willard appears in many 'new church' publications and on websites such as http://thinkexist.com.

60. Graham Tomlin, *The Provocative Church* (SPCK, 2002).

61. Austin Flannery, *Vatican II Documents: Pastoral Constitution on the Church in the Modern World* (Geoffrey Chapman, 1972), pp. 199–200.

62. Henri Nouwen, *The Road to Daybreak* (DLT, 1997), p. 98.

63. 'Strengthen for service, Lord' (trans. C.W. Humphreys 1840–1921 and Percy Dearmer 1867–1936), Hymn 306, *New English Hymnal*.

64. Well-known prayer of St Teresa of Avila (1515–82). This translation from the Spanish is found at www.rc.net/southwark/ashfordstteresa.

65. Hooper, *Daily Readings with C.S. Lewis*, p. 47.

66. Jean Vanier, quoted in Henri Nouwen, *The Road to Daybreak* (DLT, 1997), p. 31.

67. *A New Catechism* (Search Press, 1973) pp. 102–103.

68. 'My God I love thee' (trans. Edward Caswall 1814–78), Hymn 73, *New English Hymnal*.

69. John O'Donohue, *The Way*, Vol. 34 No. 4 (1994), pp. 265–272.

70. Joseph Barber Lightfoot, *Ordination Addresses 1882*, p. 48, quoted in Alfred Plummer, *International Critical Commentary on II Corinthians* (T&T Clark, 1956), p. 185.

71. Ole Hallesby, *Prayer* (IVP, 1973), p. 67.

72. Rowan Williams, 'Traditional and Emerging Church', Presidential Address at General Synod, York, 14 July 2003, from: www.archbishopofcanterbury.org.

Enjoyed

this book?

Write a review—we'd love to hear what you think.
Email: reviews@brf.org.uk

Keep up to date—receive details of our new books as they happen.
Sign up for email news and select your interest groups at:
www.brfonline.org.uk/findoutmore/

Follow us on Twitter @brfonline

By post—to receive new title information by post (UK only), complete the form below and post to: BRF Mailing Lists, 15 The Chambers, Vineyard, Abingdon, Oxfordshire, OX14 3FE

Your Details
Name _____
Address_____
_____
Town/City _____ Post Code _____
Email _____

Your Interest Groups (*Please tick as appropriate)	
☐ Advent/Lent	☐ Messy Church
☐ Bible Reading & Study	☐ Pastoral
☐ Children's Books	☐ Prayer & Spirituality
☐ Discipleship	☐ Resources for Children's Church
☐ Leadership	☐ Resources for Schools

Support your local bookshop
Ask about their new title information schemes.